P9-DMQ-894

PACKERS ESSENTIAL

Everything You Need to Know to Be a Real Fan!

Rob Reischel

TRIUMPH
BOOKS
CHICAGO

Library of Congress Cataloging-in-Publication Data

Reischel, Rob, 1969–
    Packers essential : everything you need to know to be a real fan / Rob Reischel.
    p. cm.
    ISBN-13: 978-1-57243-735-7
    ISBN-10: 1-57243-735-9
    1. Green Bay Packers (Football team)—History. 2. Green Bay Packers (Football team)—Miscellanea. I. Title.

GV956.G7R45 2005
796.332'64'0977561—dc22

                                                              2005044017

This book is available in quantity at special discounts for your group or organization. For further information, contact:

Triumph Books
542 South Dearborn Street
Suite 750
Chicago, Illinois 60605
(312) 939-3330
Fax (312) 663-3557

Printed in U.S.A.
ISBN-13: 978-1-57243-735-7
ISBN-10: 1-57243-735-9
Design by Patricia Frey
All photos courtesy of AP/Wide World Photos except where otherwise indicated

To my gorgeous wife, Laura, who's fantastically patient with my crazy schedule. To my beautiful new daughter, Madison. And to my mother, Sherry, the most positive person anyone could ever imagine meeting. You all mean more to me than you'll ever know.

Contents

Foreword

There is nothing in sports quite like being a Green Bay Packer. As soon as you put on that green and gold uniform, you immediately become part of something special, something unique, something legendary.

The fans are as passionate as any in America. The history and success are virtually unparalleled. It's the best story sports has going—and it's been that way for decades now.

I spent nine years playing for the greatest franchise in sports—nine of the best years of my life. We won five world championships in that time. We won the first two Super Bowls. We won historic, unforgettable games like the Ice Bowl. I played with some of the greatest men and teammates ever assembled. And I played each of those years under the finest coach football has ever known: Vincent Thomas Lombardi.

The city, the fans, and the Packers experience were all so good to me that I couldn't leave. I have lived in Wisconsin and have been in the bar business in and around Green Bay since 1961. I currently have Fuzzy's #63 Bar & Grill, along with Fuzzy's Tickets and Tours in Green Bay. As you can imagine, there's typically just one topic of conversation when you enter Fuzzy's, and it's football.

That's commonplace throughout Green Bay, though. Whether you're at the grocery store, in line for the movies, or walking into church, people want to talk Packers, Packers, and more Packers.

Which is one reason I love this book so much. It takes you on a joyride through the history of this great organization. There are unique stories and wild tales from the days of Lambeau through the Lombardi years up until today.

The author talked to roughly 100 individuals who have either played for or coached the Packers at some point. And that will give you—the fans—great insight and a unique perspective on the history of the Green Bay Packers.

Like I said, there's nothing in sports quite like being a Green Bay Packer. And this book shows exactly that. I hope you enjoy it as much as I did.

—Fuzzy Thurston

Introduction

Jan Stenerud was on a plane to Green Bay late in the 1980 football season.

He'd already spent 13 fantastic seasons in Kansas City, revolutionizing the place-kicking position and etching his name among the game's all-time greats. As Stenerud's plane crept closer and closer to Austin Straubel Airport, the legendary kicker had but one thought.

"I just kept asking myself, 'What in the world am I doing?'" he said.

Four years later, when Stenerud was leaving Green Bay for good, he had his answer.

"I've said many times, I had a long and wonderful career," said Stenerud, the only kicker in the Pro Football Hall of Fame. "But if I hadn't gotten a chance to play in Green Bay, I would have missed out. It's so special and so important up there. Looking back, I'm thrilled I got that opportunity. I enjoyed it so much."

Most who pass through the smallest city in professional sports, one that's home to roughly one hundred thousand people, feel the same way. That's because they realize something awfully fast: football in Green Bay, Wisconsin, is life.

The Packers have a waiting list for season tickets of about sixty-seven thousand. That means that if you put down your two-year-old son's name today, he figures to get a call when he's in his midthirties.

The Packers have an annual scrimmage against themselves—and folks pack Lambeau Field to watch a glorified practice. Fans often take their vacations the same weeks as training camp so they can watch their heroes up close and personal. And the tailgate parties and festivities during a home-game weekend are legendary.

Anyone who has ever stepped foot in the fishbowl that is Green Bay will quickly tell you there's nowhere else quite like it.

"You try to think back and look at it sometimes and it's kind of like landing in Chicago at night," said former Packers defensive back Doug Hart. "You know how you have all the lights and all the people, it's kind of like a fantasy. Well, that's how Green Bay was. It was kind of like a fantasy. Sometimes I question if I was really there because it was such a great time in my life."

To this day, the Packers remain the most unique team and one of the most spectacular stories in sports.

The Packers don't have an owner. Instead they have 111,921 shareholders who have purchased stock at four different times in franchise history when the Packers encountered tough times. None of the stockholders has ever received a nickel on their initial investment. And to ensure someone can't take control of the team, no one person can own more than two hundred thousand of the nearly 5 million shares that exist.

In an era of big-money owners like the New York Yankees' George Steinbrenner and the Dallas Mavericks' Mark Cuban, the Packers are governed by a seven-member executive committee and a board of directors. Oh yeah, and the fans.

"This is a unique place," Packers president Bob Harlan said. "People want to be a part of it. It's goose-bump time when they get here."

That's for sure. Since Green Bay was founded in 1919, it has produced one goose-bump moment after another.

The Packers have won 12 NFL championships—more than any other team in football. And they've been involved in some of the most memorable games in league history, such as the "Ice Bowl" and the "Instant Replay" contest.

Green Bay had arguably the greatest coach the sport has ever known in Vince Lombardi. And the Packers' 21 Hall of Fame inductees rank second behind Chicago's 26.

Lambeau Field, Green Bay's home stadium, has been in continuous use longer than any professional sports stadium except Boston's Fenway Park and Chicago's Wrigley Field. And a trip to Lambeau Field, which was renovated earlier this decade, is a virtual pilgrimage to the holy land for Packers fans everywhere.

In 2002 Harris Interactive named Green Bay America's favorite football team, and in 2003 the Packers tied Dallas for the top honor.

"I can't tell you how much I liked Green Bay," said former Packers tackle Norm Masters. "It's one of the meccas of sports and just a great place to play football. I think about how lucky I've been to play there."

Through the years, there have been countless unforgettable moments, remarkable players, and sensational teams. The following pages provide an in-depth look at those.

Enjoy the ride, much as Stenerud and many others have.

The Green Bay Packers: How They Began

Take a walk through the *Green Bay Press-Gazette* newsroom, drop the name George Calhoun, and you're likely to get a lot of blank stares.

"I don't think it means anything anymore," said Tony Walter, the paper's sports editor from 1977 to 1984 and again from 1994 to 1996. "I'd say a very low percentage know the history there."

Then they're missing out on quite a tale. Were it not for Calhoun and Earl "Curly" Lambeau, there may have never been a National Football League team in tiny Green Bay, Wisconsin.

Back in 1919 Calhoun was the sports editor at the *Press-Gazette*. One day, Calhoun bumped into Lambeau, a player he had covered when Lambeau was a star athlete at Green Bay East High School. The two men began talking about forming a football team. And amazingly, that's how the Packers got their start.

Calhoun ran a story in the *Press-Gazette* a short time later targeting local athletes to try out for the team. On August 11, 1919, the group met in the *Press-Gazette*'s editorial room, and a football team was organized.

Shortly thereafter, Lambeau's employer, the Indian Packing Company, agreed to put up the money for uniforms and allowed the team to practice on company ground. Naturally, the nickname "Packers" developed.

That modest beginning started a remarkable relationship between Lambeau and the Packers. The 21-year-old Lambeau became player/coach when Green Bay played its first game against the Menominee North End A.C. in 1919. It wasn't until 1949 that he resigned.

Because the Packers didn't play their first league game until 1921, Lambeau's official career statistics don't begin until that time. But over the next 29 years, Lambeau compiled a remarkable 212–106–21 record

1

IF ONLY . . . Terrell Davis' migraine headache in Super Bowl XXXII had lasted a couple of hours longer, Green Bay may have repeated as champions. Instead, Davis returned after sitting out most of the second quarter and finished with 157 yards and three touchdowns to lead the Broncos to a 31–24 win.

(.656) with the Packers and led Green Bay to six world championships. He also enjoyed a nine-year playing career, in which he threw 24 touchdown passes and had 110 career points.

"Curly was fairly strict with his players," said 88-year-old Hal Van Every, one of a few ex-Packers still alive who played under Lambeau. "He was pretty tough on the guys, but that's the way we wanted it back then. We thought that was the best way to win."

The Packers won almost as soon as Lambeau got them started. In 1919 Green Bay went 10–1 playing nonleague games against teams throughout Wisconsin and upper Michigan. That team outscored its opponents 565–12, as Lambeau led a high-flying offense that loved to throw the ball.

The team played its games at Hagemeister Park, a vacant lot next to Green Bay East High School. The Packers didn't charge for games back then, instead staying afloat by having patrons "pass the hat."

By 1921 the Packers had become so successful that Lambeau got the backing of two officials at the packing plant, which had been bought out by the Acme Packing Company. They purchased a franchise in the American Professional Football Association, which later became the NFL.

Green Bay became a league powerhouse under Lambeau by the late twenties. Between 1929 and 1931, the Packers compiled a 34–5–2 record and won three straight championships, which were decided back then by league standings, not postseason games.

Green Bay's first postseason game came in 1936, when the team defeated the Boston Redskins, 21–6, for the title at the New York Polo Grounds. After the Packers lost the championship to the New York Giants in 1938, they had revenge the following season and defeated New York, 27–0, for the title in a game played at Milwaukee's State Fair Park.

Lambeau guided the Packers to another championship in 1944, when they topped the Giants, 14–7, at the Polo Grounds. But Lambeau left for the Chicago Cardinals after the 1949 season when he lost an internal power struggle with the executive committee.

Lambeau had some amazing accomplishments while in Green Bay, though. He became one of just six coaches to earn at least two hundred career wins. He coached seven Packers who reached the Hall of Fame. He started daily practices in the twenties and began flying to road games in 1938. And, of course, one of the most hallowed stadiums in all of sports was later named after him.

"He was very interesting," said 88-year-old Bob Kahler, who also played under Lambeau. "He had a great personality, very outgoing and friendly and really a players' coach.

"He was a very flamboyant guy," Kahler continued. "He was a flashy dresser, and he drove a Lincoln Zephyr. But he expected you to do a job and made sure you did it. He was really a great coach."

The *Press-Gazette*, which played such a large role in the Packers' ever getting off the ground, had an extremely unique relationship with the team back then.

Calhoun worked as the team manager, publicist, and traveling secretary from 1919 to 1947. And he wrote about the team in the *Press-Gazette*, as well.

Andrew B. Turnbull was the general manager of the *Press-Gazette*, as well as the Packers president from 1923 to 1927. Turnbull helped keep the Packers afloat in 1922 when financial woes hit the team. Then in 1923 Turnbull convinced local businessmen to purchase stock in the team and turn it into a nonprofit corporation, something the Packers still are today.

Needless to say, with the presence of Turnbull and Calhoun in the newsroom, the Packers could do nothing wrong on the pages of the *Press-Gazette*.

John Walter, Tony's father, was the paper's sports editor from 1935 to 1941. Tony recalls stories from his dad about how he was instructed to cover the team.

By the NUMBERS

Zero—The number of owners the Green Bay Packers have. The Packers are the last remaining publicly owned pro sports team, with 4,749,925 shares and 111,921 stockholders. No dividends are issued.

Head coach E. L. "Curly" Lambeau gets a lift from his players following the 1944 championship game against the Giants at the Polo Grounds.

"Dad kept a diary about the team back then," he said. "And he wrote in there that he was under orders from Turnbull to never criticize the Packers. I know Dad and Curly had their clashes back then. But when it came to putting things in print, he could never criticize the team."

For the most part, the paper served largely as a mouthpiece for the organization until the seventies. Of course, most of what was taking place on the field was positive, as the Packers won six titles under Lambeau and five world championships in the sixties under Vince Lombardi.

Then in 1974, Lee Remmel left his job as the *Press-Gazette*'s sports editor to accept a position as the Packers' director of public relations, and a new leaf was turned over at the paper.

Shortly thereafter, *Press-Gazette* reporters stopped flying on the team plane. The paper's managing editor, Larry Belonger, saw to it that the kid gloves were taken off. And young reporters like Cliff Christl and later Bob McGinn were hard, but fair.

"There was a pivotal moment in the seventies when Cliff [Christl] had a big blow-up with [head coach] Bart [Starr], for something he had written," Tony Walter said. "And Bart said that unless the *Press-Gazette* apologized, we'd no longer be allowed to fly on the team plane. Well, we didn't back down. That was a big moment."

Today, the paper's biggest moments usually come via the Packers.

The *Press-Gazette* throws an enormous percentage of its sports resources into the Packers. And they combine forces with the *Appleton Post-Crescent* to battle the state's largest paper, the *Milwaukee Journal Sentinel*.

TRIVIA

Which team broke Green Bay's 25-game home winning streak in 1998 and by what score?

Answers to the trivia questions are on pages 162–163

"Our philosophy is you can't have too much Packers," said Mike Vandermause, the paper's current sports editor. "We joke that if Brett Favre burps, that's a story. And it's not because of our history with the team. It's because this is a professional football team in a city of one hundred thousand people and it's owned by the fans. And that's unique."

Much like the vision Lambeau and Calhoun had all those years ago.

Hutson—the Best Ever?

Bob Kahler's favorite Don Hutson moment remains etched in his memory, even though Kahler is 88 years old and the play took place more than 60 years ago.

Kahler remembers a time during the 1944 season when the Green Bay Packers were less than a yard away from scoring. Defenses keyed on the brilliant Hutson, often putting two and three defenders on the Green Bay receiver.

Hutson lined up on the right and drew plenty of traffic when he came inside. Instead of continuing his route, though, Hutson grabbed the goal post—which was in the front of the end zone back then—pivoted, and spun back to the outside.

Hutson was wide open and hauled in one of his 99 career receiving touchdowns.

"Hutson was just amazing," said Kahler, one of just two ex-Packers still alive who played with Hutson. "You could call him the Jordan of our sport back then."

That certainly seems like a fair comparison.

When debating the greatest receiver of all time, the discussion typically includes Jerry Rice and Hutson. And the conversation ends there.

Hutson set 18 NFL records during his career, which lasted from 1935 to 1945. Amazingly, 10 of those marks still stand six decades later.

Hutson was credited with inventing pass patterns, creating routes such as Z-outs, buttonhooks, and hook-and-gos. His world-class speed helped change the way the passing game was viewed. And several so-called experts have named him the greatest player of the 20th century.

"If you missed Hutson, you missed one of the greatest ever," said 88-year-old Hal Van Every, who played with Hutson in 1940 and 1941. "He had that speed, and he had some pretty good passers back then.

"But they could just lay the ball out there and he'd run under it. There was nothing better than old Don Hutson. He was just an amazing player."

That's for sure.

TRIVIA

In which playoff game did Green Bay score its most points?

Answers to the trivia questions are on pages 162–163

Just consider some of the NFL records Hutson still holds today. He once scored 29 points—in a single quarter. He led the NFL in scoring five times and led the league in overall TDs on eight occasions.

Hutson led the NFL in receptions eight times, and he had the most consecutive seasons leading the league in overall TDs (four on two occasions). He led the league in receiving touchdowns nine times and receiving yards seven times. He was a nine-time All-Pro, and he received the NFL's Joe F. Carr Trophy as the league's most outstanding player in 1941 and 1942.

"Guys today like Randy Moss couldn't carry his shoes," said Van Every, a back who threw his share of passes to Hutson. "I don't think the league will ever have anyone like him again."

Hutson's brilliance on the field is just part of the story, though. Those who knew Hutson well say as good as he was on the field, he was even better off it.

"He was a terrific person," Kahler said. "A good family man and very unassuming. Nothing like the wide receivers of today. Oh God, no. Not all this 'Get me the damn ball!' baloney."

"He wasn't a shouting guy," added Van Every. "I don't ever remember him popping off. He did his job, did it well, and everyone respected him. He was a great teammate."

The Packers came perilously close to never having Hutson suit up for them, however.

A star at Alabama, Hutson signed with both Green Bay and the Brooklyn Dodgers. But Joe Carr, the league's president, ruled that the

By the NUMBERS

Four—Number of times Green Bay avoided financial collapse. The team was in dire straits in 1921, 1922, 1934, and 1950, but it received financial support from the community each time.

Packers' contract with Hutson was postmarked 17 minutes earlier than Brooklyn's. And Hutson became a Packer.

It was one of the best things that ever happened to the franchise.

Hutson had 9.5-second speed in the 100-yard dash and punished defenses with it. In just his second game, he burned the hated Chicago Bears for an 83-yard touchdown pass in a 7–0 Green Bay win, giving his new employer a glimpse of what was to come.

Hutson, who also doubled as a defensive back and a kicker, went on to set NFL records in touchdown receptions and 200-yard receiving games (he had four). During two different seasons, he averaged more than 23 yards per reception, and he averaged a whopping 16.4 yards per catch for his career.

But Hutson's contribution to the game extended far beyond just numbers. When he first broke into the league, most teams had predominantly running offenses. But Hutson changed that in Green Bay. He helped to make the Packers one of the league's most dangerous passing outfits. And he changed how offense was played.

"Teams used to line their ends in tight," Kahler said. "But teams always had two or three guys on him. Then [Packers coach]

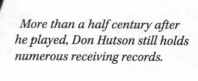

More than a half century after he played, Don Hutson still holds numerous receiving records.

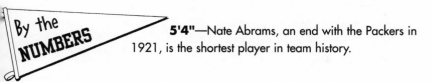

5'4"—Nate Abrams, an end with the Packers in 1921, is the shortest player in team history.

Curly [Lambeau] got smart and started splitting the ends out. He was the first one to do that. Defenses didn't know how to react. It really helped the running game and really helped Hutson."

For that reason some of Hutson's better years were in the twilight of his career. In 1942, his eighth year in the league, Hutson set career highs in receptions (74), yards (1,211), and touchdowns (17). In fact, Hutson accounted for exactly 46 percent of his career receptions, touchdowns, and receiving yards over his final four years in the league, a time during which several players were also called away to World War II.

Hutson's No. 14 was retired in 1951, making him the first Packer to receive that honor. He was named to the NFL's All–50 Year Team and 75th Anniversary Team.

Then in 1994 the Packers built a $4.7 million state-of-the-art indoor practice facility. Its name? The Don Hutson Center. Three years later, arguably the greatest Packer ever passed at the age of 84.

"I think he's the best ever," Kahler said. "I really do. I've never seen anybody come around who was any better than he was."

From Rags to Riches

From a financial standpoint, these are salad days for the Green Bay Packers.

When the 2004 fiscal year ended, the Packers had $84 million in cash reserves. The revenues in that year were $179.1 million, which ranked 10th in the National Football League.

And with the recent renovation of Lambeau Field, Green Bay is positioned to be one of the NFL's most prosperous franchises for years to come.

My, how things have changed.

Several times in the franchise's early days, Green Bay flirted with financial ruin. And no one understands that better than Stan Heath.

Heath was the Packers' first-round draft choice in 1949 and the fifth overall selection that year. Heath played one year in Green Bay; then the Packers told him they couldn't afford him.

"It was just one of those deals where they weren't going to honor my contract," said Heath, who played quarterback. "They were having trouble financially and told me and some other players they couldn't honor the contract."

When the 1949 season ended, Green Bay was in a financial crisis. A war between the NFL and the All-America Football Conference left the Packers so financially strapped they lost two of their three number one draft picks to the AAFC between 1946 and 1948.

The team eventually worked its way out of financial ruin thanks to an Old-Timers game on Thanksgiving Day, 1949, that raised $50,000 and a giant stock sale in 1950 that raised another $125,000.

But that wasn't enough to keep Heath around, which left the local boy extremely disappointed.

TOP TEN — Most Sacks

1.	68.5	Reggie White	1993–1998
2.	58.5	Kabeer Gbaja-Biamila	2000–present
3.	55.0	Tim Harris	1986–1990
4.	41.5	Ezra Johnson	1982–1987
5.	36.0	Tony Bennett	1990–1993
6.	32.5	Bryce Paup	1990–1994
7.	32.0	Vonnie Holliday	1998–2002
8.	26.0	Santana Dotson	1996–2001
9.	25.5	Robert Brown	1982–1992
10.	24.5	Sean Jones	1994–1996

Heath had grown up in Milwaukee and attended Shorewood High School before beginning his collegiate career at the University of Wisconsin. When he longed for more playing time, he transferred to the University of Nevada, where he starred and eventually became Green Bay's first-round draft choice.

Heath played the 1949 season for $15,000, which he calls "tip money" today. The Packers saw such a contract as excessive, though, and they knew they couldn't afford to keep it on their books if they were to continue to stay afloat. Near the end of the year, Green Bay told Heath he'd have to rework his deal if he wanted to stay. And although he would have preferred to remain in his home state, Heath opted to play in the Canadian Football League, where he stayed the next five years.

"There's no animosity on my part toward them," said Heath, who's retired today and living in Alaska. "It was just one of those things. They were having a lot of problems, and they just couldn't pay everybody. I never missed a check, but things weren't going well for the organization at that time."

It wasn't the only time Green Bay flirted with financial disaster.

In 1922 bad weather and poor attendance left the team in trouble. But

TRIVIA

Has Green Bay ever posted a shutout in the postseason?

Answers to the trivia questions are on pages 162–163

Team president Bob Harlan unveiled the new logo for Lambeau Field in May 2001, just weeks before launching the $295-million redevelopment plan that has been a huge success for the franchise.

local merchants raised $1,000 in the team's first stock offering, and Green Bay became a publicly owned corporation.

In 1934 a fan won a $5,000 verdict after falling from the stands and suing the Packers. After the insurance company went out of business, the Packers went into a receivership and appeared ready to fold. But more than $15,000 was raised in a stock drive, and Packers president Lee Joannes paid $6,000 to settle the case, then convinced the courts to end the receivership period.

In 1949, the year Heath played in Green Bay, the Packers organized an intrasquad game that raised $50,000 and helped the team stay afloat. But the biggest boom came in 1950, when another stock drive raised $118,000 and put the team on solid financial footing.

By then, however, the Packers had cut ties with several players like Heath. Much to their chagrin.

"I would like to think I could have done some good things," Heath said. "We didn't have much of a season the year I was there. But I enjoyed it a lot and wish it could have worked out a little differently."

It certainly has worked out well for the Packers since. Huge television deals, revenue sharing, and a salary cap have allowed the league's smallest city to prosper. And the recent renovation of Lambeau Field has provided a cash flow the Packers had never seen before. It's a complete 180-degree turn from the days when Heath played.

"The first thing that I'm proud of, and I don't want to apologize for being successful . . . , [is that] when we went after the stadium, we said that we've got to do this stadium because it's going to help us in revenue," Packers president Bob Harlan said. "It's going to keep us competitive. It's going to keep us a viable part of the National Football League. It's going to bring visitors to Green Bay from literally around the world. And it has done all of those things. Everything we said to the voters in 2000 has come true. So I don't want to apologize for us making money."

Nor should he. For the Packers, it's a much better situation than the franchise's early days.

The Forgettable Fifties

Today, National Football League coaches get virtually no sleep before games.

They watch film, looking for that last little weakness to exploit in their opponent. They spend time tidying up the game plan. And they stress about what Sunday holds.

Scooter McLean wouldn't fit very well in today's coaching world. Then again, he didn't fit very well as Green Bay's coach back in 1958 either.

"Oh man," former Packers wide receiver Gary Knafelc sighs when McLean's name is mentioned. "Scooter would play poker with the players the night before the game. And what was worse is he wasn't even good at it. [Max] McGee would just take him to the cleaners."

McLean's one year running the team was the low point during a decade of despair for the Packers. From the time Curly Lambeau left at the end of the 1949 season to the time Vince Lombardi took over in 1959, Green Bay was a miserable 32–74–2, didn't have one winning season, and had only two years it didn't finish below .500.

Gene Ronzani, who replaced Lambeau, went 14–31–1 from 1950 to 1953. Lisle Blackbourn followed with a 17–31 record from 1954 to 1957, then McLean went a laughable 1–10–1 in his only year in charge.

"Those days were just miserable," said linebacker Tom Bettis, Green Bay's number one draft choice in 1955 and a Packer until 1961. "There was always talent there. Just not a lot of discipline."

In fairness to Ronzani, he walked into a less-than-desirable situation. The Packers had gone just 5–19 in Lambeau's final two years and were facing bleak financial times that didn't allow them to keep their established players.

Ronzani, a former Chicago Bears star, took over as coach and vice president when Lambeau left for the exact same positions with the Chicago Cardinals. After a stock drive netted $118,000, the Packers were on more stable ground financially, but they didn't get any better on the field. The Packers' best season under Ronzani was a 6–6 campaign in 1952. And he went just 2–5–1 against the Chicago Bears, Green Bay's biggest rival.

Finally, with two games left in the 1953 season—one in which Green Bay finished 2–9–1—Ronzani resigned. Hugh Devore and McLean were named the interim coaches for the final two games, both of which Green Bay lost.

"Ronzani was a nice fellow," said Fred Cone, a fullback and kicker who played in Green Bay from 1951 to 1957. "But there was a lot of player movement back then, and he was highly suspicious that guys would take our offense back to [Chicago Bears coach George] Halas. So during meetings, he'd hold up the plays on a big cardboard sheet. And he'd only hold it up long enough for you to write down what your job was. His way of presenting things wasn't real good."

"Ronzani was kind of a weird guy," said Billy Grimes, a Packers halfback from 1950 to 1952. "One day you were his fair-haired boy, and the next day you were dirt. You never knew what to expect. He was difficult to understand.

"But we were kind of like a farm team of the Bears back then. Still, that was always the game. Halas would send spies to Green Bay to watch us practice, so we'd set up trick stuff, then never use it in the games. We'd set up crazy things just to try and fool them."

Things didn't get much better under Blackbourn, who had been the coach at Marquette University. Like Ronzani, Blackbourn had but one year (1955) in which his team played .500 ball.

"Blackbourn wasn't as likable as Ronzani," Cone said. "But he was a real sound fundamental coach. I don't want to say anything bad about Ronzani, but Blackbourn knew football much, much better. It's just that

IF ONLY . . . Green Bay had selected Barry Sanders instead of Tony Mandarich with the number two overall pick in 1989. Had that happened, Green Bay's backfield through much of the nineties would have been Sanders and quarterback Brett Favre.

By the NUMBERS

21—Packers in the Pro Football Hall of Fame. That total is surpassed by only Chicago, which has 26. The list includes:

Earl L. "Curly" Lambeau, founder, player, head coach, vice president (1919–1949)

Robert "Cal" Hubbard, tackle (1929–1933, 1935)

Don Hutson, end/defensive back (1935–1945)

Johnny "Blood" McNally, halfback (1929–1933, 1935–1936)

Clarke Hinkle, fullback (1932–1941)

Mike Michalske, guard (1929–1935, 1937)

Arnie Herber, quarterback (1930–1940)

Vince Lombardi, head coach and general manager (1959–1967), general manager (1968)

Tony Canadeo, halfback (1941–1944, 1946–1952)

Jim Taylor, fullback (1958–1966)

Forrest Gregg, tackle (1956, 1958–1970)

Bart Starr, quarterback (1956–1971)

Ray Nitschke, linebacker (1958–1972)

Herb Adderley, cornerback (1961–1969)

Willie Davis, defensive end (1960–1969)

Jim Ringo, center (1953–1963)

Paul Hornung, halfback (1957–1962, 1964–1966)

Willie Wood, safety (1960–1971)

Henry Jordan, defensive tackle (1959–1969)

James Lofton, wide receiver (1978–1986)

Reggie White, defensive end (1993–1998)

when you don't have a lot of talent, there's not much you can do. That was our biggest problem."

Blackbourn also didn't get along well with the Packers executive committee. That, along with the fact that Green Bay was struggling to win games, led to his firing after the 1957 campaign.

"He was a very good coach who didn't get along with the executive committee," Knafelc said of Blackbourn. "I think he would have won if they would have allowed him to go along."

"He was a good coach. His personality was a little peculiar," Jim Temp, a defensive end from 1957 to 1960, said of Blackbourn. "He was a little man and had trouble communicating with the players. He certainly didn't put the fear of God in you."

Compared to McLean, though, Blackbourn seemed like a bona fide dictator.

McLean, a popular assistant, was promoted to head coach after Blackbourn was fired. But McLean's preference was to hang out with his players rather than to discipline them. There were no curfews or dress codes. There were no repercussions for missing a meeting. And players took full advantage of the overmatched McLean.

It wasn't until Lombardi, still known as Saint Vince in Green Bay, arrived on January 28, 1959, that things began to turn around for the Packers after a disastrous decade.

TOP TEN

Most Games Played

1.	223	Brett Favre	1992–present
2.	196	Bart Starr	1956–1971
3.	190	Ray Nitschke	1958–1972
4.	187	Forrest Gregg	1956, 1958–1970
5.	181	LeRoy Butler	1990–2001
6.	174	William Henderson	1995–present
7.	167	Ed West	1984–1994
8.	166	Willie Wood	1960–1971
9.	164	Robert Brown	1982–1992
10.	162†	Larry McCarren	1973–1984
	162†	Ron Hallstrom	1982–1992

"He didn't exercise any authority, and we just had a disastrous season," Temp said of McLean, who was fired after just one year. "The players just didn't have any respect for him."

Not only was Green Bay's .091 winning percentage the worst in team history, the Packers weren't even competitive most Sundays. Baltimore beat them 56–0. The 49ers steamrolled them, 48–21. They were outscored 382–193 on the year and lost their last seven games.

About the only significant contribution McLean made to Packers history was establishing Green Bay's training camp home. That year, the Packers stayed at nearby St. Norbert College during camp, and they've been there ever since.

Still, that little bit of good didn't come close to offsetting the bad.

"It was a miserable year," Knafelc said. "Nobody took Scooter seriously. How could they?"

All of that changed the following year with the arrival of Vincent Thomas Lombardi, who's still known as Saint Vince in Green Bay. Lombardi inherited a group that had some talent but needed discipline. They needed to be molded into winners.

"What was happening was we had some talent," said Norm Masters, a Packers tackle from 1957 to 1964, "but we needed someone to get us organized."

Lombardi was that man—and he helped take some of the sting out of the forgettable fifties.

"The early days were miserable in many respects," Bettis said. "And 1958 was a real downer [when the Packers went 1–10–1]. All hell broke loose that year.

"We had some talent; we just needed someone strong and disciplined who treated the players fairly. Lombardi was obviously that guy. He did a magnificent job."

TRIVIA

Which former Super Bowl–winning quarterback was on Green Bay's roster during its 1996 Super Bowl season?

Answers to the trivia questions are on pages 162–163

Saint Vince

Bart Starr will never forget the day he knew things were about to change in tiny Green Bay, Wisconsin.

It was 1959, and the Packers had just made little-known Vince Lombardi their next head coach. Green Bay hadn't had a winning season since 1947 and was coming off a 1–10–1 campaign.

But Starr, the Packers' quarterback, knew the losing was about to end. Starr was 20 minutes into his first meeting with his new head coach, and he was downright giddy. At his first opportunity, Starr ran to the phone to call his wife, Cherry.

"I said, 'Honey, we're going to begin to win,'" Starr recalled.

That proved to be an enormous understatement. Over the next nine years, Lombardi led Green Bay to five world championships, including two Super Bowl victories. He compiled a remarkable .758 winning percentage (including playoffs) in Green Bay. Even Lombardi's name is attached to the Super Bowl trophy.

Bring up a discussion regarding the greatest coach the game has ever seen, and arguing someone other than Lombardi is a tough sell.

"He was the best coach ever, and I think few would question or argue that," said Jerry Kramer, a Packers guard from 1958 to 1968. "He always had you ready to go, mentally and physically. All you had to do was watch him and emulate him, and you'd be ready to play. Plus, he was just a tremendous teacher, very thorough. It was an honor to play for him."

It's easy to see why. Lombardi, who had never been a head coach, changed everything about the football culture these Packers had grown accustomed to.

Lombardi demanded discipline, focus, and ultimately perfection. He changed the Packers' attitudes and their mind-set. He even

By the NUMBERS

13—Packers head coaches (listed in order of regular-season winning percentage):

	Name	Years	Record	Pct.
1.	Vince Lombardi	1959–1967	89–29–4	.746
2.	Mike Holmgren	1992–1998	75–37	.670
3.	Earl "Curly" Lambeau	1921–1949	209–104–21	.657
4.	Mike Sherman	2000–2005	57–39	.594
5.	Ray Rhodes	1999	8–8	.500
6.	Phil Bengtson	1968–1970	20–21–1	.488
7.	Dan Devine	1971–1974	25–27–4	.482
8.	Bart Starr	1975–1983	52–76–3	.408
9.	Forrest Gregg	1984–1987	25–37–1	.405
10.	Lindy Infante	1988–1991	24–40	.375
11.	Lisle Blackbourn	1954–1957	17–31	.354
12.	Gene Ronzani	1950–1953	14–31–1	.315
13.	Ray "Scooter" McLean	1958	1–10–1	.125

redesigned Green Bay's uniforms and bought every player a jacket, slacks, and a tie.

"He told us we're not some stumblebums," former tackle Bob Skoronski said of Lombardi. "He wanted us to look as good as the doctors or the lawyers in town.

"His philosophies weren't just those of a football coach. He was like a father and a teacher. We were all part of something special, and we didn't even know it was happening."

Really, Lombardi and the Packers were a match made in heaven.

Before Lombardi arrived in Green Bay, he was at his wit's end, unsure whether a head coaching opportunity would ever present itself. The Brooklyn native had been a standout guard at Fordham University, part of that school's legendary "Seven Blocks of Granite" offensive line. When Lombardi's playing days ended, he was an assistant coach at Army and then for the New York Giants.

He had built a reputation as one of the top assistants in football and was seen as the potential successor to Jim Lee Powell, when the Giants coach retired. But in January 1959, all Lombardi knew was that he was beginning his off-season job at Federation Bank and

Trust, and deep down he feared he was destined to remain a lifelong assistant coach.

Green Bay, meanwhile, had become a league laughingstock. And the days of Curly Lambeau, who led the Packers to six world championships in 31 years before leaving after the 1949 season, seemed like decades ago.

Jack Vainisi, the Packers' personnel manager who assembled much of the talent with which Lombardi would later win, was the first to call. Vainisi helped steer Packers president Dominic Olejniczak in the direction of Lombardi.

The two sides eventually agreed on a contract that paid Lombardi $36,000 per year for five years and gave him complete control of the football operations. It was the best money the Packers ever spent.

"He had prepared for that job for a long time," former Green Bay tackle Norm Masters said of Lombardi. "He came in and he had a plan, and we used his criteria as a leader. He demanded that people respond to his program, and he convinced us that we'd be successful if we listened to him. And we were."

Vince Lombardi cheers his team to the 1965 National Football League championship against the Cleveland Browns.

"He set standards to create a winner, and he knew what the end result would be. From day one, you knew from how he presented himself that he had a strong grasp. And as we started to win, we all became believers."

From the day Lombardi walked through the front door, things were different. The loosey-goosey atmosphere that existed under Scooter McLean was gone for good, replaced by one of efficiency, structure, and organization.

No more excuses. No more screwups. No more failing.

The players quickly learned that "Lombardi time" meant you arrive for meetings 10 minutes early. Practices were brutal compared to those with past Packers coaches, sending some like Dave "Hawg" Hanner to the hospital. But they were also crisp, without a wasted second.

Lombardi instituted his signature play, the Packer sweep. He scaled the playbook back, running fewer plays with more variations of each one, believing less is more if it's executed to perfection. And he did all he could to make his team tougher—both mentally and physically—than its foe.

Slowly but surely, Lombardi's chase for perfection began to yield results. And when his first team closed the 1959 season with four straight wins, Green Bay finished with a 7–5 mark and its first winning campaign in 12 years.

In 1960 Lombardi guided Green Bay to the NFL championship game, where the team fell to Philadelphia, 17–13. But the Packers made amends the following year, defeating Lombardi's old New York Giants team, 37–0, for the title.

In 1962 the Packers not only repeated as world champions, they also produced one of the best years in NFL history. Green Bay went 13–1 that season, then toppled the Giants, 16–7, for the title.

"If I could put one word on it, it would be discipline," Skoronski said of the key to Green Bay's success. "Discipline in our study. Discipline in the execution. Discipline in how we prepared. There was a chain around us all the time.

TRIVIA

Which member of Green Bay's 1996 Super Bowl championship team won an NCAA championship the previous year?

Answers to the trivia questions are on pages 162–163

Memorable Quotes

From the Lips of Vince Lombardi

"Fatigue makes cowards of us all; high physical condition is vital to victory."

"A winning football team must avoid mistakes with a passion; treat mistakes with a vengeance."

"The harder a man works, the harder it is to surrender."

"Football is a game of inches, and inches make a champion."

"Desire is a hate for your opponent."

"Maybe winning isn't everything, but it sure comes way ahead of whatever is second."

"The goal line is the moment of truth; there is no room for a timid person there."

"Good fellows are a dime a dozen; aggressive leaders are priceless."

"Confidence is contagious, so is a lack of confidence."

"Our greatest glory is not in never failing, but in rising ever time we fail."

"Plus, [Lombardi] got us in the kind of physical shape that when the game was decided in the fourth quarter, we were in shape to do it. He brought an attitude about winning and a professionalism that we lacked, and if you weren't prepared for every play, it was a calamity."

After a two-year drought, Lombardi's Packers were back to championship form in 1965. Green Bay and Baltimore tied for the Western Conference crown with 10–3–1 records and squared off for the right to advance to the NFL championship game.

The Packers got three field goals that afternoon from Don Chandler, including a controversial one that forced overtime. To this day, the Colts insist the kick sailed wide right. But the referees saw it differently, which helped Green Bay go on to a 13–10 win. The following week, the Packers held Jim Brown, the game's greatest player, to 50 yards and downed Cleveland, 23–12, for the title.

The Packers repeated in 1966, defeating Dallas, 34–27, for the NFL championship, then hammering Kansas City, 35–10, in Super Bowl I. Before the next season began, Lombardi knew it would be an enormous challenge to rally his team to play at such a high level again. So he reached into his bag of motivational ploys and sold his aging team on the fact that they could make history.

"The one thing that really stands out is when we were going for three straight championships; that was something that had never been done before," said Tom Brown, a Packers cornerback from 1964 to 1968. "And he told us we wouldn't appreciate it until we were 50 years old. And the Old Man—we always used to call him the Old Man—was right. But he was over and above a coach. What he stood for and to be on those teams was incredible."

The 1967 season proved to be rather incredible, too. With some of the Packers' key players getting long in the tooth, many sensed it could be a final go-around, and they made it memorable.

Green Bay defeated Oakland 33–14 that year to win Super Bowl II. But when people think of that season, they remember the NFL championship game.

In a contest that became known simply as the "Ice Bowl," Starr scored from one yard out with 13 seconds left to give Green Bay a 21–17 win over Dallas. That game, played on a day when the windchill dipped to 46 degrees below zero, was the culmination of Green Bay's greatness in the sixties.

"Coach Lombardi was so special, and the biggest reason why was his ability to always motivate people," said Boyd Dowler, a Packers wide receiver from 1959 to 1969. "He motivated the same people over a nine-year period, and the nucleus was almost always the same, and you never saw a real letdown."

Lombardi's management of people was almost as important as his X's and O's. He understood he could get in the face of some players, while others needed a softer approach.

For the most part, Lombardi knew exactly what buttons to push. Now and again, though, his instincts failed him. In the early sixties, the *Chicago Tribune* had just published a story calling Kramer and Fuzzy Thurston the best pair of guards in football. Later that same week in practice, a Packer sweep went nowhere and Lombardi went ballistic.

"He came running up screaming, 'The best pair of guards in football, my [expletive],'" said Kramer, who also scored 156 points as the Packers' place-kicker in 1962–1963. "And I was already playing hurt. I had broken two ribs the week before in San Francisco, and I just snapped. I was dead set on punching him in the mouth. I got off the pile, and I thought, 'OK, I'll be suspended. I'll get docked my salary. And I'm sure I'll get traded.'

"And I just said, '[expletive] it!' I'm going to hit him. I was so angry and so out of control. So I walked over by him, and he wouldn't look at me. He just stayed turned away.

"Finally I got over my anger and decided to walk the sidelines. Well, after five or six minutes, just the right amount of time for me to cool off, Lombardi came down and patted me on the shoulder and rubbed my hair. It was good for both of us that I didn't hit him."

That's for sure. Like many of his teammates, Kramer may not have always liked Lombardi's harsh, dictatorial ways, but the Packers all seemed to realize Lombardi was making each and every one of them better.

"I was definitely one of his whipping boys," former tight end Gary Knafelc said. "He screamed at me constantly. I didn't like the guy, and physically he frightened me. But I'll take everything he gave me. I wish I had another five years with him because he made me a much better player."

By the end of the 1967 season, however, Lombardi's days of making the Packers better players were over. He resigned as head coach but stayed on as general manager.

Needing a new challenge, Lombardi accepted the head coaching job in Washington in 1969 and took over a team that hadn't had a winning season in 14 years. To the surprise of no one, Lombardi's first team in Washington went 7–5–2.

It proved to be his only team in Washington, as Lombardi died of cancer in September 1970.

"Obviously, like everybody, I held him in the highest regard," Bob Long, a Packers wide receiver from 1964 to 1967, said of Lombardi. "He altered my life dramatically and for the better. He changed my football life and my business life, and I learned a lot from him. I learned to be mentally disciplined. I learned that in business, everything needs to be done correctly. I learned that when I had a meeting, you get there 20

Guard Jerry Kramer (No. 64) helped carry Coach Lombardi off the field after their team won Super Bowl II over the Raiders in 1968.

minutes early. I learned to set goals. I learned so much from Lombardi; it's incredible."

Lombardi's accomplishments remain among the most incredible in league history. And those who got a chance to suit up for him know how fortunate they truly were.

"I could never, ever not think about Green Bay and Coach Lombardi whenever I had problems to resolve," said Doug Hart, a Packers defensive back from 1964 to 1971. "For so many years, we competed under the highest pressure possible and maintained our poise. That really helps you later on in life."

"The big thing is that we played as a team," said Masters. "You never really saw any friction of any type. And if you think about it, what people remember are the great teams. It's because of that team, not any individuals, that we still get such great notoriety. And Lombardi always preached that whole team concept. He was the kind of guy who pushed you hard and you didn't realize it until afterward, but he made you better than you thought you could be."

Which is why he'll forever be remembered as one of the greatest coaches ever to have lived.

The Best of the Best

There's a reason the smallest city in professional sports is known as Titletown. The Green Bay Packers have won 12 world championships since their inception, more than any other franchise in professional football.

Curly Lambeau, who coached the Packers from 1919 to 1949, oversaw six of those titles. Vince Lombardi led Green Bay to a remarkable five crowns during his nine years as coach. And Mike Holmgren guided the Packers to the Super Bowl championship in the 1996 season.

All of those teams were memorable in their own right. But most who have watched the Packers through the years agree that no group in franchise history was better than the 1962 bunch.

"That team was incredible," said former tight end Ron Kramer, who spent seven years in Green Bay. "Everybody was in their prime; everybody had a great year."

And Green Bay's opponents felt the wrath.

The Packers went 13–1 during the regular season that year, the second-best winning percentage in team history. They defeated the New York Giants 16–7 to win their second straight NFL championship, and Green Bay outscored its opponents 415–148 that season, a margin of nearly 3-to-1.

"That probably was the best year we had during the Glory Years," quarterback Bart Starr said. "Everything just kind of aligned right that season. We avoided injuries that season. It was our fourth year with Vince, so we all knew just what he wanted. And a lot of our core guys were in their prime. It was an incredible season."

Boy, was it ever.

TRIVIA

Green Bay drafted players in 2001, 2002, and 2003 who had played for NCAA championship teams. Name those players.

Answers to the trivia questions are on pages 162–163

Running back Jim Taylor bulldozed for 1,474 yards and 19 touchdowns that year, two marks that stood for 41 years before Ahman Green broke them in 2003. Starr had his best season yet, completing 62.5 percent of his throws and finishing with a 90.7 passer rating.

The dynamic pass-catching duo of Max McGee and Boyd Dowler combined for 98 receptions, more than any pair of receivers in the Lombardi era. And the offensive line of left tackle Bob Skoronski, left guard Fuzzy Thurston, center Jim Ringo, right guard Jerry Kramer, and right tackle Forrest Gregg was unparalleled.

Green Bay's defense included future Hall of Famers in linebacker Ray Nitschke, defensive end Willie Davis, safety Willie Wood, and cornerback Herb Adderley. That group allowed just 10.6 points per game and forced a remarkable 59 turnovers.

"That was a great football team, probably the best of any we had there," Wood said.

He'd get very few arguments.

Green Bay outscored its first three foes 100–7 that year and was challenged just twice while storming to a 10–0 start. The only blemish on the Packers' sensational season came in a 26–14 setback at Detroit on Thanksgiving.

A loss at Detroit on turkey day wasn't unusual for Green Bay, though. The Packers and Lions met every Thanksgiving between 1951 and 1963, and Green Bay went just 3–9–1 in those games.

"We'd always go to Detroit on Thanksgiving, and we'd almost always lose over there," said Dowler, a Packers wide receiver from 1959 to 1969. "But we thought that year was going to be different."

By the NUMBERS

Five—Packers who have been named MVP or Player of the Year in the league. The list includes Don Hutson (1941–1942), Paul Hornung (1961), Jim Taylor (1962), Bart Starr (1966), and Brett Favre (1995–1997).

TOP TEN

Most Seasons Leading Team in Touchdowns

1.	11	Don Hutson	1935–1945
2.	5†	Verne Lewellen	1926–1930
	5†	Jim Taylor	1959, 1961–1964
	5†	Sterling Sharpe	1989–1990, 1992–1994
5.	4	Ahman Green	2000–2003
6.	3†	Billy Howton	1952, 1956–1957
	3†	Donny Anderson	1967, 1970–1971
	3†	Barty Smith	1976–1977, 1979
	3†	Paul Coffman	1979, 1983–1984
	3†	Dorsey Levens	1996–1997, 1999

It wasn't. But Lombardi insisted immediately afterward that a loss at that time of the year wasn't a terrible thing for his team.

"I think we'll be a better football team for having lost this one," Lombardi told reporters after the game. "That business about an undefeated season was a lot of bunk. Nobody in his right mind could have expected it. The loss had to come sometime, but I honestly didn't think it would come today. No more pressure. This loss will make a better team out of us. Look out for us now."

Lombardi couldn't have been more prophetic. Green Bay won its final three games, including road games against San Francisco and the Los Angeles Rams, and won the Western Conference by two games over Detroit.

That set up a repeat of the 1961 NFL championship, in which the Packers defeated the New York Giants, 37–0. The game was played in brutal conditions at Yankee Stadium, with winds gusting up to 40 miles per hour and the game-time temperature at 13 degrees.

But Green Bay beat both the Giants and the elements, 16–7. Nitschke, the game's eventual MVP, had an interception and recovered two fumbles. Taylor set a playoff record with 31 carries and scored a touchdown. Jerry Kramer banged home three field goals. The Giants' only score came when they blocked a McGee punt for a touchdown.

Paul Hornung carries the ball in the Packers' home win over Detroit during the 1962 season. Green Bay's only loss of the season would come against the Lions in Detroit on Thanksgiving Day.

Afterward Lombardi sent all of his players a letter thanking them for a glorious season. Most Packers surveyed no longer have a copy of that letter, but former offensive tackle Norm Masters kept his.

"I'm one of the few guys who saved that letter," said Masters, who played with the Packers from 1957 to 1964 and lives in Detroit. "Even Vince Lombardi Jr. asked me once where I got it, and I said, 'Your dad sent it out to the team.' It's really special to me."

In the letter, Lombardi opened by saying that words will never express his gratitude. He talked of how success is more difficult to live with than failure.

Lombardi said the Giants tried intimidating the Packers, but Green Bay prevailed, thanks to its mental toughness. He said the Packers are made up of men of great character, and he reminded the players there is no substitute for victory. Then, he told each player that he was going to send them a color television.

"A color TV was big time back in those days," Masters said. "But really, that letter has meant a lot to me. I've used it many times in my life, and I used so much of what Coach Lombardi taught us."

TRIVIA

In which round was Bart Starr selected in the 1956 draft?

Answers to the trivia questions are on pages 162–163

Of Green Bay's other championship units, a few could also claim to be the best Packers team of all time.

The 1929 bunch went 12–0–1, was the only undefeated team in franchise history, and outscored its opponents 198–22. But that team played in an era when the game was more recreational than a full-time occupation. Also, Green Bay didn't have to win a postseason game back then. Instead, the Packers were awarded the championship based on having the league's best record.

The 1966 team was nearly as dominant as the 1962 group. That year the Packers went 14–2 overall and outscored their foes 335–163.

Then in 1996 Green Bay went 16–3 and won Super Bowl XXXI. That team finished first in the league in total offense and defense and outscored its opponents 456–210.

But from top to bottom, the 1962 team is one that's hard to match—not only in Packers annals, but also in the history of the NFL.

"I look back now and it's incredible how close we were to going unbeaten," Wood said. "That was an incredible football team. There won't be many like that one again."

Taylor-Made for Success

The leading rusher in Green Bay Packers history wasn't the fastest back you'll ever see. He wasn't particularly shifty or elusive. But Jim Taylor would run you over, then look for you again the next time he had the ball. And if an opposing defender didn't have a few of his teammates nearby, Taylor might take him for a ride.

It's why Taylor will be remembered as one of the game's greats and one of the brightest stars during the Packers' "glory years."

"He was a tough son of a gun," former Packers offensive lineman Bob Skoronski said of Taylor.

Skoronski would get few arguments.

Taylor came to Green Bay out of Louisiana State University as the 15th pick in the 1958 draft. He left as the most prolific rusher in Packers history and the proud owner of a career that earned him induction into the Pro Football Hall of Fame in 1976.

During his nine seasons in Green Bay, Taylor rushed for a team-record 8,207 yards, a mark current Packers running back Ahman Green (7,103) is closing in on.

Taylor eclipsed 1,000 yards rushing in five straight years (1960–1964), a team record he currently shares with Green (2000–present). Taylor led the NFL in rushing in 1962 with 1,474 yards, another team record, which stood for 41 years before Green erupted for 1,883 yards in 2003. And Taylor led the Packers in rushing seven seasons (1960–1966), a total equaled by only Clarke Hinkle, who did so between 1932 and 1941.

Taylor, who played in five Pro Bowls, had 26 games with more than 100 yards rushing, also a team record. He averaged 4.53 yards per carry, which ranks third behind Ahman Green's 4.60 and Gerry Ellis' 4.58.

Taylor's 91 career touchdowns rank second in team history to Don Hutson (99), who played 11 years in Green Bay. And Taylor's 19 touchdowns in 1962 were a club record until 2003, when Green scored 20 times. Green had two additional games to do so, though.

"He was such a tough back," said former right guard Jerry Kramer, who helped clear many of Taylor's holes. "One guy wasn't bringing Jimmy down. You needed more than that."

Of all Taylor's accomplishments on the field, though, perhaps the one he remains most proud of is his fumbles—or lack thereof. In 2,166 career touches, both rushing and receiving, Taylor had just 34 fumbles. That equates to just one fumble every 63.7 touches, a mark that stood until Detroit's Barry Sanders shattered it with one fumble in every 83.3 touches.

The greatest rusher in Packers history, Jim Taylor races upfield with a Bart Starr pass during the NFL championship game on January 1, 1967.

By the NUMBERS

11—Number of Packers general managers

Curly Lambeau	(1919–1949)
Gene Ronzani	(1950–1953)
Verne Lewellen	(1954–1958)
Vince Lombardi	(1959–1968)
Phil Bengtson	(1969–1970)
Dan Devine	(1971–1974)
Bart Starr	(1975–1980)
Tom Braatz, executive VP/FB operations	(1987–1991)
Ron Wolf	(1992–2001)
Mike Sherman	(2001–2005)
Ted Thompson	(2005–present)

"I was very conscious to maintain my hold on the ball," said Taylor, who lives in Baton Rouge, Louisiana. "I was always very conscientious about maintaining the football. And that's a record I always cherished. I feel I was above average in maintaining the football."

Taylor was above average in every aspect of the game. He blocked with reckless abandon. And he had great hands out of the backfield, leading the Packers in receptions (41) in 1966, his final year with the team.

Throw in the fact that he operated behind one of the greatest offensive lines ever assembled and the passion that Packers coach Vince Lombardi had for the running game, and you can see why Taylor excelled.

"I was clearly running behind the best offensive line in football," said Taylor, who was also inducted into the Packers Hall of Fame in 1975. "And Coach Lombardi stressed that part of the game more than anything. We were going to run the ball 65 percent of the time or so, and [quarterback] Bart [Starr] was only going to have to throw it about 15 times a game.

"But as I look back, I can say I feel good about the contribution I made to the Packers era and the Lombardi era. I feel good about it."

Taylor had more games to feel good about than most players would dream of. But the one that stands above others remains the 1962 NFL championship game against the New York Giants at Yankee Stadium.

The game-time temperature was 13 degrees and falling, and with winds gusting up to 40 miles per hour, many players said the conditions were worse than the legendary Ice Bowl. The field was also hard and frozen, and when players fell, pieces of dirt cut them like glass.

In the first quarter, Taylor was drilled by Giants linebacker Sam Huff, tore up his elbow, bit his tongue, and was swallowing blood the rest of the half.

"That had never happened to me before," Taylor said. "It was rough."

But so was Taylor. After getting stitched up at halftime, Taylor played on and played exceptionally well. Despite his multiple injuries, the fact that his hands were nearly frozen, and that the Giants were gunning for him, Taylor was the impetus in Green Bay's 16–7 win. He finished with 31 carries for 85 yards and a touchdown, as the Packers won their second straight title.

"Did everything I could to that [expletive]," Huff recalled later. And Taylor just stared at him and said, "That's your best shot?"

"That was just a brutal, brutal football game," Taylor said. "We didn't wear gloves back then, so that made it even worse. But we accepted it and just went out and did our job."

After years of doing his job as well as anyone in the NFL, Taylor and Lombardi reached an impasse. Prior to the 1966 season, the Packers had given youngsters Jim Grabowski and Donny Anderson big contracts to be their backfield of the future. Taylor, always one of the stauncher negotiators among Packers players, became determined to play out his contract and go in search of big money himself. So after the 1966 campaign, he returned home and played one frustrating year with the New Orleans Saints.

Although Taylor and the expansion Saints struggled on the field in 1967, the move proved beneficial. After his career ended, Taylor spent 18 years working as a color commentator and later a scout for the Saints.

TRIVIA

What is the current capacity of Lambeau Field?
A. 60,890
B. 68,307
C. 72,601
D. 78,413

Answers to the trivia questions are on pages 162–163

He and Lombardi also patched up their differences, and when Taylor went into the Hall of Fame, he asked Marie Lombardi to give the introductory speech.

"After Vince went to the Redskins, we had dinner one night," Taylor recalled. "And after that, everything was great again."

Almost as great as Taylor's days with the Packers.

"When I got drafted by Green Bay, I didn't know anything about it or where Green Bay even was," Taylor said. "But for me, it turned out to be a stroke of luck because they needed running backs, and Coach Lombardi came along the next year. At the time, I just said I'll go there and do my job. And I think things worked out fine."

Anyone who was fortunate enough to see Taylor play would certainly agree.

Ringo Sets the Record Straight

Jim Ringo wants to set the record straight once and for all. No, Ringo didn't want out of Green Bay. No, Ringo's trade was not premeditated. And most important, the Packers' All-Pro center didn't enter Vince Lombardi's office back in 1964 with an agent as has been widely speculated through the years.

"That's the thing I really want people to know," said Ringo, a Packer from 1953 to 1963 who was named to Pro Football's Hall of Fame in 1981 and has his name on the Packers' Ring of Fame inside Lambeau Field. "I didn't have an agent. They were only for the elite players back then. I really don't know how that story got going. Sometimes people create their own stories, and such fallacies are not good things."

Through the years, the tale of Jim Ringo has become almost legendary. Packers mythology tells it as such: before the 1964 season, Ringo was unhappy with his annual salary of $17,500 and went to coach and general manager Vince Lombardi to ask for a $7,500 raise. Just one catch. Ringo brought a player agent with him.

Although agents are status quo today, they were new to the sporting world at that time, and Lombardi was downright insulted by the mere presence of such creatures. So after Ringo, who had played in seven Pro Bowls and started 126 consecutive games for Green Bay, issued his demands, Lombardi excused himself. A few minutes later he returned and told Ringo and his agent to talk to the Philadelphia Eagles, the team to which Lombardi had just traded Ringo, about a raise.

Although Ringo was indeed traded, Lombardi's move wasn't made in haste. Lombardi had determined that Ringo was nearing the end of his career and was working on a deal with the Eagles for months. When Lombardi decided Ringo's demands were too high, he completed a trade

Jim Ringo (No. 51) opens a hole for Jim Taylor during a 49–17 rout of the Cleveland Browns on October 15, 1961. Photo courtesy of Robert Riger/Getty Images.

that brought linebacker Lee Roy Caffey and a first-round draft choice (which eventually became fullback Donny Anderson) to Green Bay for Ringo and fullback Earl Gros.

As the tale grew through the years, it only added to the Lombardi lore. Bring in an agent, deal with the consequences. Just ask Jim Ringo.

The last person who was going to squash such a tale was Lombardi himself, who relished the tough-guy role.

"There are a lot of stories about how the trade existed," said Ringo, who is retired and living in Chesapeake, Virginia. "But I never had an agent that day."

Despite winning NFL championships in 1961 and 1962, Ringo wasn't crushed to exit Titletown. His four children and wife at the time were all in eastern Pennsylvania, and Ringo said his wife wouldn't come to Green Bay.

TRIVIA

Which year did the Packers begin playing games at Lambeau Field?

Answers to the trivia questions are on pages 162–163

So if Ringo was going to be traded anywhere, Philadelphia was the ideal spot.

"My life was back on the East Coast," said Ringo, who played four more seasons for the Eagles and would stretch his string of consecutive starts to 182, then an NFL record. "So it was nice to get back there. I commuted back and forth every day and never had to move out of the house. It was ideal for me. Who knows, maybe Vince did it for my blessing."

That's doubtful, but make no mistake about it, Ringo was a blessing for the Packers. Green Bay selected him in the seventh round of the 1953 draft out of Syracuse, and Ringo started from day one.

Ringo played for Gene Ronzani's final team that year, one that struggled to a miserable 2–9–1 record. He then played four years under Lisle Blackbourn in which Green Bay went 17–31, then one season for Scooter McLean in which Green Bay was an abysmal 1–10–1.

But in 1959 Lombardi arrived, and things changed in a hurry.

"Everything was completely different," Ringo said. "This man came in a complete unknown and turned everything around.

"The man was just one of the greatest coaches you'll ever find, a great philosopher and a great man. Any phase, he was there."

And the results were fantastic. By Lombardi's third year, Green Bay won its first of back-to-back NFL championships and had gone from doormat to dominator.

"That experience was just incredible," said Ringo, a captain on those title teams. "To be a champion in a community that small was something else. No matter where you went, somebody knew you. You'd

By the NUMBERS   6'9"—Brennan Curtin, an offensive tackle whom Green Bay selected in the sixth round in 2003, is the tallest player the Packers have ever drafted.

TOP TEN

Most Touchdowns in a Season

1.	20	Ahman Green	2003
2.	19	Jim Taylor	1962
3.	18	Sterling Sharpe	1994
4.	17	Don Hutson	1942
5.	16	Jim Taylor	1961
6.	15†	Paul Hornung	1960
	15†	Jim Taylor	1964
8.	13	Billy Howton	1952
9.	12†	Don Hutson	1941, 1943
	12†	Javon Walker	2004

walk down the street and people would say hi and want to talk about the Packers."

Ringo's play gave them plenty to talk about. His blocking was essential to Green Bay's signature play, the Packer sweep. And he did it all despite weighing somewhere between 215 and 220 pounds, although he was listed in the 230-pound range.

"I'd probably be a safety today," joked Ringo, who was named to the sixties All-Decade Team. "But only I knew what I could and couldn't do versus guys. I understood there were certain challenges and only you could make them go right or wrong."

One challenge has been to once and for all set straight the facts of his infamous trade. "I know it makes for good copy, but there was no agent," Ringo said. "I promise you that."

Never Beat the Boss

Vince Lombardi's temper was legendary. He'd yell and scream. He'd rant and rave. And nothing would set him off quite like losing. No one understands this better than Babe Parilli.

Parilli, Green Bay's first-round selection in 1952 and the Packers' quarterback for four seasons between 1952 and 1958, went golfing with his new coach before the 1959 campaign. On that day, Parilli made one gigantic mistake: he beat Lombardi.

"We were only playing for a dollar," said Parilli, who's retired and living in Denver. "But afterward, he threw the dollar at me and said, 'That's the last dollar you'll ever make from me.' And before the season started, he cut me."

Parilli admits there were other factors involved, most notably a young quarterback on the roster named Bart Starr. But if anything, it allowed Parilli the opportunity to go elsewhere and flourish. And that he most certainly did, moving to the American Football League and quarterbacking Oakland, Boston, and the New York Jets between 1960 and 1969.

By the time Parilli's career was finished, he had thrown for nearly 23,000 yards and 178 touchdowns, highlighted by the 1964 season in which he threw for 3,465 yards and 31 touchdowns for the Boston Patriots.

"I had a good career," Parilli said. "It was a good run."

Parilli wouldn't have minded if his run in Green Bay had lasted longer. He came out of the University of Kentucky having learned under the legendary Bear Bryant and quarterbacks coach Ermal Allen, who later was the quarterbacks coach of the Dallas Cowboys. Parilli was a tremendous student of the game and would play a board game with

TOP TEN

Consecutive Seasons Leading Team in Scoring

1.	9	Ryan Longwell	1997–2005
2.	7	Don Hutson	1939–1945
3.	5t	Verne Lewellen	1926–1930
	5t	Fred Cone	1953–1957
	5t	Chris Jacke	1989–1993
6.	4t	Ted Fritsch	1946–1949
	4t	Paul Hornung	1958–1961
8.	3t	Don Chandler	1965–1967
	3t	Chester Marcol	1972–1974
	3t	Jan Stenerud	1981–1983
	3t	Al Del Greco	1984–1986

Bryant every day in which they would simulate game situations and try to outsmart each other.

"We did that for three years," Parilli remembered. "By the time I left, the board was worn out."

But Parilli was just getting warmed up. In his rookie season in Green Bay, he threw for 1,416 yards along with 13 touchdowns and 17 interceptions as the Packers went 6–6.

The following year, Parilli threw just four touchdowns with 19 interceptions, and Green Bay dipped to 2–9–1. Afterward, Parilli left to fulfill an Air Force commitment, and Packers head coach Gene Ronzani was fired.

"I loved Gene," said Parilli, who wore three different uniform numbers (10, 15, and 16) during his time in Green Bay. "I think Gene would have been great in today's game because the players loved him. We just didn't have any talent."

Parilli was traded to Cleveland and played there in 1956. He returned to Green Bay in 1957 and had some shining moments in a Packers uniform. He threw the first touchdown pass in the new City Stadium (later named Lambeau Field) to Gary Knafelc in 1957. And in 1958, he outperformed Starr, throwing for 10 touchdowns and 1,068 yards.

Parilli also sensed the Packers were beginning to put together a foundation for future successes. Although Green Bay went 4–19–1 under Lisle Blackbourn and Scooter McLean in 1957–1958, several of the key cogs that would later produce five world championships in seven years were being acquired.

And Parilli felt Lombardi was walking into an awfully good situation.

"It was hard back then to build a team," Parilli said. "Today, you've got free agency. But back then, it took time for your talent to come around.

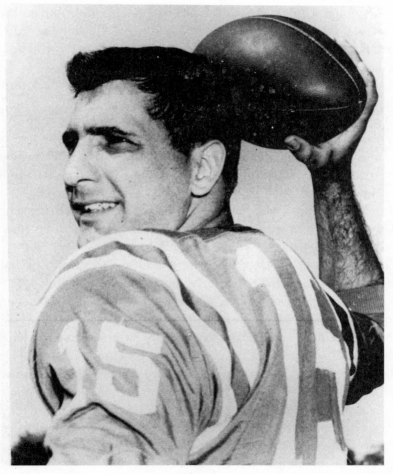

Babe Parilli poses as a member of the Boston Patriots, where he landed after Coach Lombardi cut him.

"And I really thought [Lombardi] came into a good thing. He made some good moves, but he also came into a good situation."

Parilli could also tell his situation in Green Bay wasn't a particularly solid one. Although Parilli quarterbacked Lombardi's first victory, a 24–17 preseason triumph at San Francisco in 1959, he knew he was squarely in Lombardi's doghouse.

"He was kind of a sore loser, like all of us were, I guess," Parilli said of Lombardi. "I remember a game where we came down on the opening drive and got to about the 10-yard line. I took a timeout and went and asked him what to do. And he never called a play. He said, 'Run it, throw it, whatever.' I went back to the huddle and [Paul] Hornung asked me, 'What'd he say?' And I said, 'You're going to get the ball and run it into the end zone.' And that's what he did. He scored on the play."

Maybe that was the first indicator that Parilli himself had a future in coaching.

When he retired from the game following the 1969 season, he began an extremely successful coaching career. Parilli served as the quarterbacks coach for Pittsburgh and Terry Bradshaw in 1972–1973, he was the quarterbacks coach for Denver in 1977 when the Broncos went to the Super Bowl, and he later tutored Steve Grogan in New England.

Parilli was also a head coach in the World Football League in 1974–1975 and a head coach in the Arena Football League from 1988 to 1992 and from 1994 to 1997.

"I think the year we went to the Super Bowl in Denver was probably the highlight," said Parilli, who worked with the Broncos from 1977 to 1979 and has lived in Denver ever since. "I had a great time in Pittsburgh working with Bradshaw, and I really enjoyed the Arena League. But by the time I was done, I had been in six leagues as a player and a coach. I had had my fill."

Despite his untimely golfing victory over Lombardi, Parilli has never gotten his fill of Green Bay. He returns every year for Alumni Weekend, stays in touch with several of his former teammates, and looks back fondly on his time in the NFL's smallest city.

"I loved my years there," he said. "Every year when I go back, I stop and look at the old house I used to live in. Green Bay was good to me."

Even if Lombardi wasn't.

By the NUMBERS

12—Green Bay has won more world championships than any other NFL franchise. Here's a recap of each one:

1929: The Packers went 12–0–1 under Curly Lambeau. The NFL didn't play a championship game in this era; instead they awarded the title to the team with the best winning percentage.

1930: Green Bay went 10–3–1 under Lambeau (.769) and won the title based on league standing.

1931: The Packers went 12–2 under Lambeau (.857) and again won the championship because of their league-best winning percentage.

1936: Green Bay defeated the Boston Redskins, 21–6, in the championship game played at the Polo Grounds in New York. Don Hutson caught a 48-yard touchdown pass from Arnie Herber in the game's first three minutes, and Green Bay never trailed.

1939: Arnie Herber and Cecil Isbell both threw touchdown passes, and Green Bay blanked the New York Giants, 27–0, in a game played at Milwaukee's State Fair Park. The Packers intercepted six passes and held the Giants to just 164 total yards.

1944: Fullback Ted Fritsch scored twice, and Green Bay topped the New York Giants, 14–7, at the Polo Grounds. Joe Laws, Green Bay's 34-year-old halfback, set a playoff record with three interceptions and added 74 rushing yards.

1961: Bart Starr threw a pair of touchdown passes, and Green Bay routed the New York Giants, 37–0. Paul Hornung, on leave from the army, accounted for 19 points with one touchdown, three field goals, and four extra points. Green Bay's defense, meanwhile, forced five turnovers and held the Giants to six first downs and 130 total yards.

1962: Jerry Kramer made three field goals and linebacker Ray Nitschke earned MVP honors as Green Bay defeated the New York Giants, 16–7. Nitschke recovered two fumbles—one that led to a Jim Taylor touchdown—and deflected a pass that was intercepted. Green Bay ended the year 13–1.

1965: Paul Hornung ran for 105 yards and Jim Taylor had 96 as the Packers topped Cleveland, 23–12, at Lambeau Field. The Packers also held Browns star Jim Brown to just 50 yards after Brown ran for 1,544 yards during the regular season.

1966: Max McGee caught a pair of touchdown passes from game MVP Bart Starr as Green Bay defeated Kansas City, 35–10, in Super Bowl I. McGee replaced Boyd Dowler, who was injured on the first series, and caught seven passes for 138 yards. McGee had caught only four balls all season. The game was not a sellout, as more than thirty thousand seats remained empty.

1967: Bart Starr threw for 202 yards, including a 68-yard touchdown pass to Boyd Dowler, as Green Bay defeated Oakland, 33–14, in Super Bowl II. All-Pro cornerback Herb Adderley also returned an interception 60 yards for a score. The game ended Vince Lombardi's nine-year reign as Packers coach, a time in which he won six Western Conference championships, five NFL titles, and two Super Bowls.

1996: Green Bay's 29-year title drought came to an end when it defeated New England, 35–21, in Super Bowl XXXI. Desmond Howard had 244 total return yards, including a 99-yard kick return that iced the game, and earned MVP honors. Brett Favre threw for 246 yards and two touchdowns, and Green Bay intercepted Patriots quarterback Drew Bledsoe four times.

The Ice Bowl

Willie Wood never thought he'd be playing football on New Year's Eve in 1967.

When Green Bay's free safety woke up that morning, he discovered his car wouldn't start. With temperatures well below zero, Wood's battery had died. Wood didn't think the prognosis was any better for the Packers' NFL championship game that day against the visiting Dallas Cowboys.

"Never," Wood said. "I didn't think there was a chance in hell they'd make us play that day."

What fun would that have been?

Had that been the case, the most famous game in NFL history would have never taken place. One of the most memorable endings in league history wouldn't have transpired. And the Green Bay Packers might have never claimed their fifth world championship in seven years. Instead, all of the above unfolded on a day that will never be forgotten.

Not only did Green Bay defeat Dallas, 21–17, that afternoon when Bart Starr scored on a one-yard touchdown run with 13 seconds left, but they did so in some of the most miserable conditions imaginable.

The temperature at kickoff was 13 degrees below zero and minus 46 degrees with the windchill. The game was played on a sheet of ice after the field's $80,000 heating system broke—or was turned off by Packers coach Vince Lombardi as some believe.

The referees' whistles froze. One fan died from exposure, and several others were treated for frostbite. And making it even worse, Lombardi wouldn't allow anyone except linemen to wear gloves.

Immediately afterward, the game was dubbed the "Ice Bowl."

"The Ice Bowl was just incredible," said former linebacker Jim Flanigan, a rookie that season. "Lombardi wouldn't let you wear gloves, and we had cutoff long johns and just regular shirts and T-shirts.

"But once you're cold, you're cold. We'd come back to the sideline and warm up by the space heaters. But I've never been through anything like it."

No one who competed that day was ever part of something like it again. Yet the league had no intention of ever halting the game, which appeared to be a good thing for Green Bay early on.

Packers quarterback Bart Starr engineered an 82-yard touchdown drive—one he capped with an 8-yard TD pass to Boyd Dowler—on Green Bay's first possession. Then early in the second quarter, Starr and Dowler hooked up for a 43-yard scoring pass and a 14–0 lead.

Dallas closed to 14–10 by halftime, though. First, Starr was sacked and fumbled deep in his own territory, and George Andrie returned it seven yards for a Dallas score. Then the normally sure-handed Wood fumbled a punt, setting up a Dallas field goal shortly before intermission.

On the first play of the fourth quarter, the Cowboys took a 17–14 lead when Dan Reeves threw an option pass to Lance Rentzel for a 50-yard TD. It stayed that way until late in the game, when the Packers took over on their own 32-yard line with 4:50 remaining.

For this proud but aging team, the next few minutes would determine their place in history: mount a game-winning drive against Dallas' vaunted Doomsday Defense and become the first team in NFL history to win three consecutive NFL championships. Or fail, and see their dynasty come to an end.

Anyone who understood these Packers understood failure wasn't an option. Green Bay methodically marched down the field to the Cowboys' 1-yard line. But after Donny Anderson was stopped for no gain on second down, the Packers used their final timeout with 16 seconds left.

GOOD THING . . . Vince Lombardi was unable to find a head coaching position before Green Bay came calling in 1959. Lombardi failed in earlier pursuits and was thrilled to take the Packers' job that year. Nine seasons later, he had led Green Bay to five world championships.

Bart Starr (No. 15, on ground at left) plunges over the goal line for the winning score in the famously cold Ice Bowl on December 31, 1967.

Starr went to the sideline to discuss what play to run with Lombardi. The two chose a wedge play, which called for fullback Chuck Mercein to get the ball. Immediately after calling the play, however, Starr worried that Mercein might slip on the ice rink that was Lambeau Field and decided to keep the ball himself.

Right guard Jerry Kramer found a rare piece of field that wasn't iced over, came off the ball fast and hard, and immediately cut Dallas tackle Jethro Pugh. Center Ken Bowman finished Pugh off, knocking him back into a linebacker.

The fantastic double-team block gave Starr just the room he needed, and when he crossed the goal line, the Packers had one of the most dramatic victories in league history.

TRIVIA

"People always want to talk about that play. But what personifies the character and makeup of that football team was the drive," Kramer said. "That was a perfect example of what those teams were all about. On that drive, we were absolutely brilliant. Chuck Mercein, Donny Anderson, Boyd Dowler, Bart, the entire offensive line. They were all outstanding."

"In so many ways, that drive kind of summed up everything that era stood for," Starr said. "[Lombardi] always preached perfection and on that last drive, we almost had to be perfect. And we were."

Afterward the Packers rushed to the locker room hoping to warm their frozen bodies. But warming up just wasn't in the cards that day.

"When the game finally ended, everybody went in looking to take a hot shower, but all we had was cold water," Flanigan said. "All the hot water had gotten used in the bathrooms through the game. It was that kind of day."

An unforgettable day is what it was. And it made for a perfect ending to Green Bay's brilliant run in the sixties.

The Packers went on to defeat Oakland, 33–14, two weeks later in Super Bowl II. That gave Green Bay its second straight Super Bowl title and its fifth NFL championship in seven years.

But the win over the Raiders truly was secondary. What had taken place 14 days earlier, a game that will be discussed for generations to come, was the real championship that year. And it's a game that will forever be frozen in time.

"That game [against Dallas] was the focal point of everything," Dowler said. "The Super Bowl was almost anticlimactic. And I think that game against Dallas and that season was kind of the climax to the whole period."

The Ice Bowl's Unsung Hero

His statistics during the 1967 season—56 rushing yards and one reception for six yards—were about as eye-popping as beige wallpaper.

He didn't join the Green Bay Packers until midway through the year, meaning fans and teammates alike had a hard time remembering old No. 30's name.

So when the Packers were set to embark on their final drive in the now infamous Ice Bowl, who would have thought fullback Chuck Mercein would play the hero? Certainly not Mercein.

"I'm definitely not the guy most people would have picked," Mercein said.

That's for sure. While Bart Starr will always be remembered for scoring the winning touchdown from one yard out with 13 seconds left to give Green Bay a 21–17 win over Dallas in the frigid NFL championship game, the Packers would never have been in that position were it not for Mercein.

On Green Bay's 12-play, 68-yard, game-winning drive, Mercein accounted for 34 of those yards and put the Packers in position for one of the most memorable victories in franchise history. To this day, Mercein never has to break out his wallet when he's in the vicinity of Packers fans.

"It was just great to be placed in a position to make a contribution," said Mercein, who was born in Milwaukee, moved to Chicago when he was in junior high, and attended Yale. "You always hope to be up to bat with the bases loaded and two outs. That's all I could have asked."

The Packers certainly couldn't have asked for any more from Mercein. He had been placed on waivers that 1967 season by the New

York Giants, largely because he didn't see eye to eye with Giants coach Allie Sherman. And when Green Bay lost starting running backs Elijah Pitts and Jim Grabowski to injury on the same day, it moved quickly to sign Mercein.

Although Mercein started down the stretch that season, he was primarily used as a blocker. But not on the Packers' biggest possession of the year.

Coach Lombardi celebrates Bart Starr's touchdown in the Ice Bowl, which was set up in part by the unlikely heroics of Chuck Mercein.

24—Green Bay's number of postseason wins, which rank fifth through the 2005 campaign. Dallas (32), Pittsburgh (28), San Francisco (25), and Oakland/Los Angeles (25) have more playoff victories. Green Bay's .632 winning percentage in the postseason ranks third all time. The Packers are 24–14 in the playoffs and trail only the Baltimore Ravens (5–2, .714) and Carolina Panthers (6–3, .667) in winning percentage.

Mercein and the offense took the field with 4:50 left on a day when the kickoff temperature was 13 below and the windchill was minus 46 degrees. Their task? Trying to erase a 17–14 deficit.

"I still remember [linebacker Ray] Nitschke walking off the field yelling at the offense, 'Don't let me down,'" said Mercein, who was playing just his seventh game with the Packers that day. "Well, I sure wasn't going to be the one to let Nitschke down."

He didn't.

Mercein got Green Bay's initial first down on the drive with a seven-yard run around right end. After the Packers marched to the Dallas 30-yard line with 1:35 remaining, Mercein made the biggest catch of his life.

Mercein had noticed during the drive that he was being left open in the left flat. He then did something extremely rare, suggesting in the huddle that Starr look his way.

Sure enough, Mercein was free. And on a day when conditions were beyond brutal, Mercein made a fantastic adjustment, hauled in the pass, and got out of bounds after a 19-yard gain to the Dallas 11.

"Nobody talked in that huddle except Bart," Mercein said of Starr, who called all the plays. "But I told him, 'I'm open in the left flat. Look for me if you need me.' It was a tough adjustment, but I had decent hands and made a big catch."

Mercein followed that with a big run. The Packers ran a play called Give 54 that looked like a variation of the Green Bay sweep and was designed to take advantage of the aggressiveness of Cowboys Hall of Fame tackle Bob Lilly.

Starr faked the sweep, and Lilly followed the guard, leaving a huge hole for Mercein, who rumbled to the 3-yard line.

TOP TEN

Most Yards Rushing in a Career

1.	8,207	Jim Taylor	1960–1964
2.	7,103	Ahman Green	2000–present
3.	5,024	John Brockington	1971–1977
4.	4,197	Tony Canadeo	1941–1944, 1946–1952
5.	3,937	Dorsey Levens	1994–2001
6.	3,860	Clarke Hinkle	1932–1941
7.	3,826	Gerry Ellis	1980–1986
8.	3,711	Paul Hornung	1957–1962, 1964–1966
9.	3,353	Edgar Bennett	1992–1996
10.	3,165	Donny Anderson	1966–1971

"Starr made a brilliant call," Mercein said. "It was a very, very gutsy call, and I almost got in."

Mercein thought he'd get his chance to score after the Packers moved to the 1-yard line and took their final timeout with 16 seconds left. In the huddle, Starr called 35 Wedge, a play designed for Mercein to get the ball. But Starr worried that the icy conditions could lead to Mercein slipping. And without telling anyone, Starr decided to run a quarterback sneak.

Mercein got a good start and didn't slip. And when Starr kept it, Mercein was momentarily stunned. But to this day, he doesn't have a single regret with how the final play unfolded.

"Honest to goodness, I wouldn't change a thing," said Mercein, a sales trader on Wall Street who lives in White Plains, New York. "It would have been great to get the last yard. It would have been the cherry on top of the icing. But Bart was so intelligent and so smart, it was the right percentage move."

TRIVIA

Which Green Bay player has worn the most uniform numbers in his career?

A. Bernie Scherer
B. Ray Riddick
C. Travis Williams
D. Mike Michalske

Answers to the trivia questions are on pages 162–163

Going to Green Bay also turned out to be the perfect move for Mercein. And thanks to his heroics on that final drive, he went from being anonymous to being famous.

"Every minute, every second of that final drive, I can still remember it," said Mercein, who played with Green Bay through 1969. "I remember it like it was yesterday.

"Going there and playing well was such a validation of my ability. I did what I was capable of doing and helped them win a world championship. It was one of the greatest experiences of my life. Those are moments that will never be forgotten."

Just like Mercein's heroics on that final drive.

McGee's Pre-Super Bowl Rendezvous: Fact or Fiction?

Max McGee enjoyed a wonderful career for the Green Bay Packers. His 345 receptions and 6,346 yards both ranked sixth all time through 2005. He played in a Pro Bowl, was part of five world championship teams, and later was the Packers' colorful radio analyst.

But that's secondary to most people. When it comes to McGee, people want to know what really happened before Super Bowl I.

Was McGee running the streets, then hitting the sheets with a pair of stewardesses he met the night before the big game? Or was the Packers receiver tucked into his own bed getting a good night of sleep.

That depends on whom you ask.

McGee, who caught only four passes the entire 1966 season, wasn't expecting any playing time that Super Bowl. But an early injury to Boyd Dowler thrust McGee into action, and he responded with a brilliant day, catching seven passes for 138 yards and two touchdowns as the Packers routed Kansas City, 35–10.

Afterward McGee's legend grew even greater. He told reporters that he sneaked out of his Los Angeles hotel room the night before the game, met up with two stewardesses he had just met, and didn't return until the next morning.

Dave "Hawg" Hanner, a Packers defensive tackle from 1952 to 1964 and a Green Bay assistant coach from 1965 to 1982, was in charge of bed checks that night. And he insists McGee is full of hot air.

"I can promise you, he was not out before that game," Hanner said. "He told that story because it sounds good in the papers. And now he's told it so many times, he believes it himself. But I'll tell you, he was not out of his room."

McGee tells a different story and says Hanner is just trying to save face. "When Hawg stuck his head in our room, I said, 'Are you going to be checking late?'" McGee said. "He screamed, 'You damned right I am.' Then he stuck his head back in and shook it no. Well, I almost ran him over trying to get out."

McGee was notorious for such antics. He and running back Paul Hornung both loved the night life and often seemed to pay out as much in fines as they brought home.

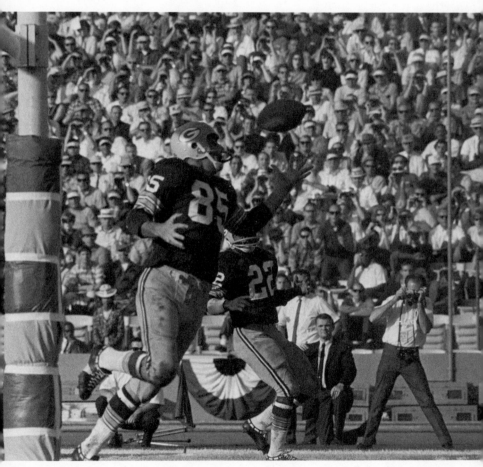

Max McGee makes a juggling catch in the end zone for one of his two touchdowns in Super Bowl I against the Kansas City Chiefs. Photo courtesy of Bettmann/Corbis.

595—Sterling Sharpe holds the Packers career record for receptions. James Lofton is second (530), and Don Hutson is third (488).

McGee believed he had virtually no shot of playing in the game. So he insists he risked the $15,000 fine, sneaked out, and played the next day on virtually no sleep.

"Hawg's one of my favorite buddies, but he's trying to cover his ass on this one," McGee said.

In their ongoing game of "He said, he said," Hanner laughs at McGee's account of the night.

"I checked him three times that night," Hanner said. "And I can guarantee you, if he got out, [Vince] Lombardi would have been on my butt. If he got out and I didn't catch him, I would have been on the ropes and Max would have been sent home. Believe me, Max didn't get out. He just thinks it makes a pretty good story."

Regardless, McGee's Super Bowl heroics made one heck of a story. Dowler left the game on the Packers' first series, and it was McGee to the rescue.

TRIVIA

Who was the first Packer to eclipse 1,000 yards rushing in a single season?

Answers to the trivia questions are on pages 162–163

He made a fantastic catch for a 37-yard touchdown for the first points of the game. Then in the third quarter, when Green Bay broke open a 14–10 affair, McGee had a 13-yard TD.

Quarterback Bart Starr was named the game's Most Valuable Player after throwing for 250 yards and two touchdowns, but the award just as easily could have gone to McGee.

"After I had scored those two touchdowns, Hornung came over to me and said, 'You're going to be the MVP,'" McGee said. "Well, I wasn't, but it was a heck of a game."

And perhaps a heck of an evening the night before, depending on whose story you believe.

Feeling the Pain

The game of football seems so glamorous. You're on television every Sunday. Commercials and endorsement deals are commonplace. Autograph hounds long for your signature.

But there is a dark side to the game, one that's rarely discussed. It's called life after football—and the brutal toll the sport takes on athletes.

No one knows this better than Willie Wood. The former Packers star safety, who was voted into the Pro Football Hall of Fame in 1989, feels like he took more hits than he gave every time he steps out of bed.

In the last few years, Wood has had four major operations, all related to his playing days. He had his right knee and right hip replaced, he had surgery on his neck to fuse the fourth and fifth vertebra, and he had lower back surgery. Even with multiple operations, though, Wood's quality of life is far from ideal.

Wood has trouble walking and uses a cane. His pain level is too high for him to play golf, one of his favorite activities. And when the weather gets cold and damp, his joints swell.

"If I had known life after football was going to be like this, I might have considered something else," said the 69-year-old Wood, who lives in Washington, D.C. "I go to the Hall of Fame things now, and as I watch the former players, 90 percent of them have a limp or some type of walking impediment.

"The game takes a toll. But I would never wish any harm to the sport or begrudge it. I love the sport, and I had a wonderful career."

That's for sure. Although Wood is paying the price today for football's physical nature, he admits he got plenty from the sport, too.

For 12 years, he patrolled center field from his free safety position as well as any player of his era. Wood, who played in Green Bay from 1960 to 1971, is second in team history with 48 career interceptions.

Wood led the league with nine interceptions in 1962 and led the Packers in picks five different seasons. Wood was selected to eight Pro Bowls and received All-NFL honors six straight years beginning in 1963.

Wood's interception in Super Bowl I is regarded by many as the turning point in Green Bay's 35–10 win. Early in the third quarter, the Packers were clinging to a 14–10 lead, when Wood intercepted Len

Willie Wood (right) was a member of the impressive Pro Football Hall of Fame induction class of 1989, which also included (from left) Mel Blount, Terry Bradshaw, and Art Shell.

Nine—Number of Packers team presidents

Andrew B. Turnbull	(1923–1927)
Ray Evrard	(1928)
Dr. W. Webber Kelly	(1929)
Lee Joannes	(1930–1947)
Emil R. Fischer	(1948–1952)
Russell W. Bogda	(1953–1957)
Dominic Olejniczak	(1958–1982)
Robert J. Parins	(1982–1989)
Robert E. Harlan	(1989–present)

Dawson and returned the ball 50 yards to set up an Elijah Pitts touchdown run.

In addition, Wood was one of the game's better punt returners. He led the league with a 16.1-yard average in 1961 and still holds the Packers record for career punt-return yardage (1,391).

After several close calls, Wood was elected to the Hall of Fame in 1989 and is one of 21 former Packers in the Hall.

"I have no regrets about my career whatsoever," Wood said. "I got more out of it than anyone would have ever imagined."

And how.

Wood, who was a college quarterback at the University of Southern California, went undrafted in large part because there were no black quarterbacks in the NFL at that time.

Wood had already made the painful decision that if he was going to play at the next level, he'd have to do so as a safety, so he began studying which teams needed help at that position. Wood then sent letters to the San Francisco 49ers, Los Angeles Rams, New York Giants, and Green Bay. He made a case for himself by detailing his collegiate career and explaining why he could be an asset. The only team he ever heard back from was the Packers. Green Bay coach Vince Lombardi wrote a letter to Wood, then sent his personnel man, Jack Vainisi, to USC to test Wood.

Wood was invited to training camp and was the last man to make the 34-man squad in 1960. He played that year for $6,500.

"I was just full of enthusiasm and so happy I made the team," Wood said. "There was always some doubt. But I didn't worry about the other stuff and gave it my best shot."

Although things were utopian for Wood on the field, they weren't as golden off it. The 1960 U.S. Census showed that there were just 128 African Americans living in Brown County, the county Green Bay is in. That accounted for just .01 percent of the total population.

Several landlords were unfamiliar with blacks and refused to rent to Wood. So he ended up living in a downtown YMCA, where his bill was $1.50 per night.

"I was just amazed and surprised," Wood said. "I had never been in a place where there weren't any black folks. But I think it was more ignorance than it was racism. People thought that if you were black, you were violent. I had a neighbor later on who really resented that I was leasing a townhouse across the street from her. But before the season ended, she was one of my best friends and remained that way."

Wood said that finding a place to rent became rather easy as the city of Green Bay began making some progress in the early sixties. But the real progress in Wood's life was on the football field.

After a year of being tutored by Emlen Tunnell, Wood took over the free safety position in 1961 and didn't let anyone else grab it until he

TOP TEN — Most Rushing Yards in a Season

1.	1,883	Ahman Green	2003
2.	1,474	Jim Taylor	1962
3.	1,435	Dorsey Levens	1997
4.	1,387	Ahman Green	2001
5.	1,307	Jim Taylor	1961
6.	1,240	Ahman Green	2002
7.	1,175	Ahman Green	2000
8.	1,169	Jim Taylor	1964
9.	1,163	Ahman Green	2004
10.	1,144	John Brockington	1973

retired following the 1971 season. In that time, Wood was part of five NFL championships and played for a coach many felt was the greatest of all time.

"Coach [Lombardi] would stand up and tell us we were making history," said Wood, who roomed for most of his career with Herb Adderley. "He'd tell us people would remember us as a great football team for years. And what he said was true. He was a great philosopher because he had the ability to see things we couldn't."

Wood lists his greatest experiences as the interception and Super Bowl I win, the 21–17 victory over Dallas in the Ice Bowl in 1967, and the 1961 NFL championship, which was Green Bay's first title under Lombardi.

"But you could pick a bunch of them," Wood said. "It was a great time."

One Wood knows he's probably paying the price for today.

"I always used to say I wish I could take more time off to do the things I wanted to do," said Wood, who coached in the NFL, CFL, and WFL after his playing days ended, before starting a company called Willie Wood Mechanical in 1982. "Now that I've got the time, I can't do that because of my ailments. I used to be so active, and now I can't do that. Like a lot of other players, I was dealt a bad hand."

After he stopped playing the game, that is.

TRIVIA

How many years did Earl "Curly" Lambeau coach Green Bay?

A. 15
B. 22
C. 29
D. 36

Answers to the trivia questions are on pages 162–163

An Era That Was Anything but Devine

Bob Hyland never meant for it to happen. To this day, though, many former Green Bay Packers joke it was the best thing Hyland ever did for the organization.

Hyland, who played center for Green Bay from 1967 to 1969, and in 1976, was with the New York Giants when they faced the Packers in the 1971 season opener. That day also happened to be Dan Devine's first game as the Packers' head coach.

It turned out to be an unforgettable day for both men.

On a rainy afternoon, Packers defensive back Doug Hart intercepted New York quarterback Fran Tarkenton. Hyland took off in pursuit of Hart and helped knock him out of bounds on the Green Bay sideline.

Because the field was soaking wet, however, Hyland couldn't stop. And he went sliding right into Devine, shattering Devine's leg in several places.

"It was just one of those fluky things," said Hyland, who lives in White Plains, New York. "It was sloppy and muddy and I couldn't stop. I kind of went careening into a bunch of people."

It wasn't until after the game that Hyland was informed that one of those people was Devine.

"When reporters came to me after the game and told me what happened, I was like, 'Jesus.' I felt awful," Hyland said. "But Devine . . . had read my comments and saw how bad I felt and sent me a telegram. He told me not to feel bad and that he always stood too close to the field anyhow. It was a crazy play."

It was also a bit of foreshadowing of how Devine's stay in Green Bay would go.

Devine came to Green Bay from the University of Missouri, where he was the Tigers' coach and athletic director. He coached the Packers from

1971 to 1974, went 25–27–4 in that time, and led Green Bay to an NFC Central title in 1972. And although several coaches in team history lost more than he did, few had stormier stints than Devine.

In that time, he made a series of atrocious personnel moves that set the franchise back nearly a decade—highlighted by his trade for John Hadl in which he gave up five picks in the first three rounds. Veteran players also had little respect for Devine's knowledge of the game, particularly when he showed Missouri game films as teaching tools and moved All-Pro guard Gale Gillingham to defense.

"When he put in the Missouri highlight film, that didn't go over real big," defensive tackle Mike P. McCoy said. "It was interesting to go in that locker room every day and see what was going to happen.

"I always thought we had a good nucleus, and if things gelled, we could have been pretty good. But it never happened, and I think a big reason is we didn't have good team unity. It was a very difficult time."

"At first, I thought it was a good idea," defensive end Clarence Williams said of Devine's hiring. "But after a while, you could see it was hard for him to make good decisions. And I also learned he was sneaky and didn't really know his X's and O's. That didn't work out well."

Not much of Devine's tenure did.

Devine, who died at the age of 77 in 2002, found the going tough in Green Bay from the start. He also seemed threatened by the past and began weeding out many of Vince Lombardi's former players.

By the NUMBERS **Six**—Number of players who played for Green Bay who won the Heisman Trophy. The list includes Bruce Smith, a back from Minnesota who won the award in 1941, then played for the Packers in 1945–1948; Paul Hornung, a back from Notre Dame who won the honor in 1956 and played for the Packers from 1957 to 1962 and 1964 to 1966; Ty Detmer, a quarterback who won the award at BYU in 1990 and played for Green Bay from 1992 to 1995; Desmond Howard, a wideout who won the honors at Michigan in 1991, then played for the Packers in both 1996 and 1999; Danny Wuerffel, a quarterback from Florida who won the award in 1996 and played for Green Bay in 2000; and Charles Woodson, a cornerback from Michigan who won the 1998 Heisman and joined the Packers in 2006.

"My only regret is I wanted to retire and play my whole career as a Green Bay Packer," said linebacker Dave Robinson, who played 10 years in Green Bay before Devine traded him in 1972. "But Devine never could learn to deal with the ghost of Lombardi, and that's why he purged the roster of Vince's guys."

And messed with what they did best. Gillingham was coming off three consecutive Pro Bowl seasons when Devine came to him before the 1972 season and told him he was moving him to defensive tackle.

"That was about as brilliant as it gets," said Gillingham, a real estate broker in Little Falls, Minnesota, since 1977. "I almost laughed. But I was a captain and stuck it out and went there. But that was about as dumb as

Bart Starr, a 16-year NFL veteran at the time, listens to rookie head coach Dan Devine during training camp in 1971.

it gets. I don't know how anybody in their right mind could have done that."

Devine, notorious for making one horrendous move after another, saw this one blow up in his face with a larger boom than most. Gillingham suffered a season-ending knee injury in just the second game of the season against Oakland when he was hit from the side.

TRIVIA

Name the only Packers coach to have exactly a .500 career winning percentage in Green Bay?

Answers to the trivia questions are on pages 162–163

According to Gillingham, though, Devine never admitted the move was a mistake.

"Dan never did anything wrong in his entire life," Gillingham said. "I could've played defensive tackle. That wasn't a problem. But with the career I was having at guard, why would you move me? That didn't make any sense.

"It was probably the dumbest thing I've ever seen. The guy was just out of place there. Maybe I think the absolute worst of him, but I was there and I had to live through it, and it wasn't good."

Gillingham said few players had good relationships with Devine. He claims the former Packers coach tried gaining support of some respected veterans by hinting about big raises when their contracts came due.

"He'd call guys in," Gillingham said. "He called me in and offered me a bribe, and I said, 'I'm not changing anything I am. I'm not changing the way I treat you or the players. I'm the captain and I represent the players.'

"It wasn't exactly offering me money. But he'd be hinting around that he'd want you to do this and want you to do that, and it was always around contract time. I don't think anybody he didn't pay off had a good relationship with him. I think pretty much everybody had a crummy relationship with him."

Perry Moss, an assistant coach at the time, agreed.

"It was a really divided ship with some Lombardi guys left and then Devine's guys," Moss said. "There was all sorts of turmoil and division within that team. It wasn't much fun."

Devine seemed to take the fun out it for many players as soon as they got to Green Bay. In 1973, Devine drafted Florida State wideout Barry Smith. When Smith went to meet Devine for the first time, he was stunned.

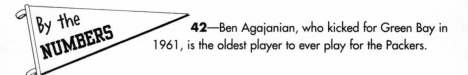

42—Ben Agajanian, who kicked for Green Bay in 1961, is the oldest player to ever play for the Packers.

"We were standing there doing a photo shoot and all that, and Devine leaned over to me and asked, 'Do you know [former New England wideout] Ron Sellers?'" Smith recalled. "I told him I did, and Devine said, 'I never liked him either.'

"I was like, 'What the [expletive] was that about?' Here I am, 22 years old and euphoric about being a first-round pick and being in Green Bay, and the coach has it out for me. But that was classic Devine. Boy, could I tell you stories."

The bottom came in 1974, when Devine traded two first-round draft picks, one second, and two thirds to the Los Angeles Rams for Hadl. Although Hadl was the reigning MVP of the National Football Conference, he was also 34 years old, was on the downside of his career, and had two forgettable years in Green Bay.

Devine didn't stick around for both of Hadl's seasons. After the Packers failed to reverse course in the 1974 season and missed the play-offs, Devine knew he was going to be fired. But before that could happen, Devine bolted for the head coaching job at Notre Dame.

"He knew what was coming," Moss said. "We were eating breakfast before the last game of the year. The staff was sitting around the table and Devine asked, 'What's the greatest coaching job in America?'

"Some guys said Oklahoma, and some said Texas or whatever. And Devine said, 'Notre Dame.' Well, sure enough, a few days later he's in South Bend being introduced as Notre Dame's coach."

While Devine landed on his feet with the Fighting Irish, his short-sighted trade for Hadl set the Green Bay franchise back several years. It also left the cupboard bare for Bart Starr, his eventual successor.

For that, many Green Bay fans never forgave him.

"I mean, history will show Dan Devine tore that team up, and he tore up that franchise," Smith said. "And I don't mean to talk bad about the dead, but let's face it, that's what he did."

Trading Away the Farm
. . . and Then Some

Three decades later, John Hadl's name still draws cringes among Packers fans. His acquisition brings back memories of a dark and depressing period in team history.

So if you mention the Hadl trade, you'll most certainly anger and annoy the Green Bay faithful.

"I think that's safe to say," said John Hadl, the quarterback acquired by Green Bay in 1974 in a deal that sent shock waves through the NFL. "That had people riled up a bit."

A bit? That's like saying the Janet Jackson Super Bowl fiasco drew mild attention from the FCC.

When the Packers started the 1974 campaign 3–3, coach and general manager Dan Devine was feeling the heat of three and a half mediocre seasons. So he mortgaged Green Bay's future and sent two first-round draft choices, one second, and two third-rounders to the Los Angeles Rams for the 34-year-old Hadl.

In Hadl's defense, he brought an impressive resume with him to Titletown. He was the reigning NFC Player of the Year after throwing for 2,008 yards and 22 touchdowns and leading the Rams to the NFC West title in 1973. Prior to that, Hadl had enjoyed 11 stellar seasons in San Diego, where he tutored under offensive mastermind Sid Gillman and threw for more than 22,000 yards.

On the flip side, Hadl was getting long in the tooth, and the Packers were a lot more than just one player away from becoming a dominant team.

"The thing I've always said is I didn't make the trade," said Hadl, who was given a raise from $90,000 to $400,000 when he joined the Packers. "I loved my time in Green Bay and really appreciated the people. But if anybody resents me, just remember, I didn't make the trade."

By the
NUMBERS

Nine—Tackle Forrest Gregg was named to more Pro Bowls than anyone else in franchise history. Gregg was named to the Pro Bowl each year from 1959 to 1964 and from 1966 to 1968. Safety Willie Wood (1962, 1964–1970) and quarterback Brett Favre (1992–1993, 1995–1997, 2001–2003) were named to eight, and wideout James Lofton (1978, 1980–1985) and center Jim Ringo (1957–1963) were named to seven.

That alone would have made him a better GM than Devine.

It quickly became apparent that Hadl wasn't the missing piece to put the Packers over the top. Hadl's play began to slip, his supporting cast was suspect at best, and it was evident rather quickly that the trade was a disaster.

"We had a lot of nice guys, and they worked awfully hard," Hadl recalled. "But we just didn't have a lot of talent."

That showed over the second half of the 1974 season. Hadl took over the starting job from Jerry Tagge, with the Packers sitting at 3–5, and sparked a little life into the team by initiating a three-game winning streak.

Shortly thereafter, though, the bottom fell out. Green Bay lost its final three games of the season, averaging just 7.7 points per contest, and finished the year 6–8.

Devine then took off for Notre Dame and was replaced by Bart Starr. Hadl returned, however, and had perhaps his most forgettable year ever in 1975.

That season, he threw for 2,095 yards and completed 54 percent of his passes. But he had just six touchdown passes and 21 interceptions, and he finished with a quarterback rating of 52.8 in Green Bay's atrocious 4–10 campaign.

That wound up being Hadl's final season in the league. The Packers, on the other hand, felt the effects of the Hadl deal for years thereafter.

By giving up the 9th, 28th, and 61st overall picks in the 1975 draft and the 8th and 39th overall picks in 1976, the

TRIVIA

Where did Vince Lombardi attend college?
A. Fordham
B. Michigan
C. St. John's
D. Duke

Answers to the trivia questions are on pages 162–163

John Hadl came to Green Bay from Los Angeles, where he was the NFC Player of the Year in 1973. Photo courtesy of Diamond Images/Getty Images.

TOP TEN — Most Rushing yards in a Game

#	Yards	Player & Game
1.	218	Ahman Green vs. Denver, December 28, 2003
2.	192	Ahman Green vs. Philadelphia, November 10, 2003
3.	190	Dorsey Levens vs. Dallas, November 23, 1997
4.	186	Jim Taylor vs. New York Giants, December 3, 1961
5.	178	Najeh Davenport vs. St. Louis, November 29, 2004
6.	176	Ahman Green vs. Chicago, September 29, 2003
7.	171	Samkon Gado vs. Detroit, December 11, 2005
8.	169	Ahman Green vs. Tampa Bay, November 4, 2001
9.	167	Billy Grimes vs. New York Yankees, October 8, 1950
10.	165	Jim Taylor vs. L.A. Rams, December 13, 1964

Packers went two years without bringing in top-notch young talent. The result? A 27–47–2 record between 1976 and 1980.

"I don't even want to go there," Starr said when asked what the trade did for his chances to succeed.

Packers fans still look back at those numbers and shudder. Hadl isn't too happy about them either.

But Hadl insists he loved everything about his time in Green Bay except the results.

"Honestly, I had a great time," said Hadl, who finished his career with 33,503 passing yards and 244 touchdowns. "I remember my first game; we were riding in on the team bus through the parking lot a couple of hours before the game, and the place was already packed.

"There were a few guys twirling a full pig over a barbecue to my right. There were three fistfights going on to the left, and everyone was having a great time. It was a neat place.

"I just hope the people up there know how much I appreciated my time there. They were great to me. I just wish we could have won more games for them."

More Packers wins would have been far more likely had the Hadl trade never been made.

An Unhappy Homecoming

In 16 years as Green Bay's quarterback, Bart Starr rarely made the wrong choice. He almost always made the right throw. He prepared for games with a vengeance and was the ultimate team leader. He was Tom Brady before the New England Patriots star was alive.

But in 1975, one of the greatest players in Green Bay Packers history made one of the poorest choices of his life.

"Going back to coach in Green Bay was the biggest mistake I ever made," said Starr, who coached the Packers from 1975 to 1983. "I was approached by the organization, and it turned out to be an enormous mistake. I was extremely disappointed. I disappointed the Packers and their fans."

Today, Starr works in Birmingham, Alabama, as chairman of Healthcare Realty Services, which provides real estate solutions to the healthcare industry.

The topic of his coaching days doesn't exactly illicit warm fuzzies. Then again, why would it?

After a brilliant career in which he won a pair of Super Bowl MVP awards and helped lead Green Bay to five NFL championships in seven years, Starr retired following the 1971 season. Four years later, he was back as coach and general manager of a franchise heading south in a hurry.

Unfortunately for Starr, the Packers never changed directions during his nine-year tenure. In that time, Green Bay went 52–76–3 and qualified for the playoffs just once.

"I accept all responsibility. I just didn't get it done," Starr said. "I haven't ever really sat and analyzed what went wrong.

16—Bart Starr, Green Bay's quarterback from 1956 to 1971, played more seasons in a Packers uniform than anyone else in franchise history. Linebacker Ray Nitschke played 15 seasons, and quarterback Brett Favre began his 15th season in 2006.

"Early on, my inexperience hurt us, but in the later years, we had some good draft choices and we were beginning to make progress. But I don't want it to sound like I'm making excuses. I just didn't get it done."

In Starr's defense, he inherited a rather dysfunctional roster. And Dan Devine's trade for over-the-hill quarterback John Hadl—one in which Devine gave up five draft picks in the first three rounds—didn't give Starr a chance to add much young talent.

"I just really thought Bart had no shot when he took over because he didn't have all those draft picks," said Mike P. McCoy, a defensive tackle in Green Bay from 1970 to 1976. "He had to try and get something back, and the pieces of the puzzle weren't all there anyhow."

It showed. Green Bay went just 31–57–2 and had only one winning season in Starr's first six years. That type of success—or lack thereof—would certainly get someone fired in today's game. But Starr was working for an extremely patient organization that wanted to see him succeed.

Green Bay began to show some signs of life, going 21–19–1 in Starr's final three years and qualifying for the playoffs in the strike-shortened 1982 campaign. But it wasn't enough to save his job. Still, Starr was the ultimate player's coach, and it's tough to find anyone who ever worked or played for him to utter a negative word.

"Playing for Bart and the person he was," former safety Johnnie Gray said, "that was tremendous."

"Bart was one of the finest people you could ever work for," said Lew Carpenter, who was Starr's receivers and passing game coach. "The only problem he had as a head coach is he listened to a lot of the wrong coaches in the organization."

Starr didn't have that problem during his legendary playing days. The son of a career air force master sergeant, Starr had the type of mental fortitude perfect to succeed under the demanding Vince Lombardi.

Getting to that point, though, was far from easy. Starr lost much of his junior and senior seasons at the University of Alabama due to back injuries, and with NFL brass leery of him physically, he wasn't even chosen until the 17th round of the 1956 draft.

Starr endured three nondescript seasons in Green Bay in which he threw 13 touchdown passes and 25 interceptions. In that time, he never could win over coaches Lisle Blackbourn or Scooter McLean.

Then Lombardi was hired, and Starr's career was never the same. Between 1961 and 1967 Green Bay not only won, it dominated. The Packers captured five championships, including three in a row in 1965, 1966, and 1967, the only team in NFL history to have won three consecutive titles.

And Starr proved to be the ultimate triggerman. By the end of Lombardi's first year, Starr had won over his new coach with sensational performances in victories over the Los Angeles Rams and San Francisco 49ers to help Green Bay close the year 7–5.

"In Bart Starr, we're going to have one of the great quarterbacks in football," Lombardi told Frank Gifford on his radio show following the season.

What Lombardi could have said was "one of the great quarterbacks in football history." While Starr's arm was far from cannon-like and he didn't scare anybody physically, few have ever been smarter. He understood all the intricacies of Lombardi's offense, recognized every complexity a defense could throw at you, and almost always made the right decision.

Starr was named to the Pro Bowl four times and was the Most Valuable Player of both Super Bowls I and II. He was the NFL MVP in 1966 when he had a quarterback rating of 105.0 and threw 14 touchdown passes and just three interceptions.

And of course, his game-winning sneak in the 1967 NFL championship game, also known as the Ice Bowl, gave Green Bay a 21–17 win over Dallas and remains one of the most memorable moments in NFL history.

Starr led the NFL in passing in 1962, 1964, and 1966 and set almost

TRIVIA

Two of the greatest players in Packers history, Don Hutson and Bart Starr, attended the same college. Name it.

Answers to the trivia questions are on pages 162–163

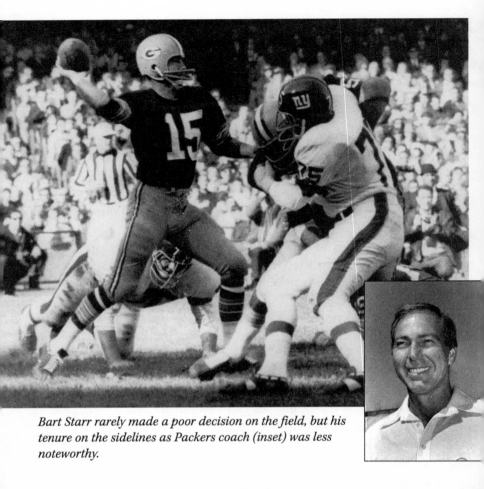

Bart Starr rarely made a poor decision on the field, but his tenure on the sidelines as Packers coach (inset) was less noteworthy.

every quarterbacking record in Packers history before Brett Favre came along. Most important, though, was the fact that Starr helped guide Green Bay to a 74–20–4 regular-season record between 1961 and 1967.

Ask Starr to talk about himself, however, and it's tougher than feeding vegetables to a toddler.

"The reason we had success is because that was a great football team," said Starr, who is among 10 players from Green Bay's Glory Years in the Pro Football Hall of Fame. "I was just one part of a great team.

"You look at the quality of players and look at the leadership we had, and it's easy to understand why we won. I was just so blessed to be in

Green Bay when I was and to be led by a gentleman [Lombardi] that's difficult to describe."

Describing just one moment as the best remains impossible for Starr. Heck, when you're choosing between the Ice Bowl, Super Bowl championships, and playing for the legendary Lombardi, you can see why it wouldn't be easy.

"I really think just the honor of playing on five championship teams in seven years is the best thing," Starr said. "Being part of a team that was so unselfish was amazing. What we were able to accomplish was very meaningful, and the fact that we were able to get it done as a team."

Although Starr admits he'll always be disappointed in how his coaching tenure turned out, he remains an avid fan of the organization. He returns to Green Bay roughly twice a year for Alumni Day and charity events. He still talks to as many former teammates as possible. And needless to say, his heroics on the field will make him a Packers legend for generations to come.

"I'd like to pay tribute to what are unquestionably the world's greatest fans," Starr said. "They are very loyal and very rabid. And I had the time of my life when I played in front of them."

Monday Night Mania

Bart Starr was never one for four-letter words or Knute Rockne–like pep talks. But October 17, 1983, was different.

Before Starr's Green Bay Packers took the field for their Monday night game against the Washington Redskins, Starr flicked out the lights and turned on an overhead projector. What his team saw was a quote from Redskins tight end Don Warren that read, "The game is going to be a rout."

The comment was one Starr had been using all week to fire up his 3–3 team. And now he went there one last time.

"Bart showed us all the quote again," said then–Packers quarterback Lynn Dickey. "But then he said something new.

"He said, '[Warren] thinks it's going to be a rout. But he never said which way. Now let's go kick some ass!' Now that was cool! Bart just never said stuff like that."

Starr's words helped Green Bay give one of the more inspired and memorable performances in the history of Monday Night Football. The Packers upended the defending Super Bowl champion Redskins, 48–47, in a game that still remains the highest-scoring contest in the history of Monday Night Football.

"Listening to people talk about that game today, you'd think about two hundred fifty thousand people were there that night," Dickey said. "Almost everyone I talk to tells me they were there."

They wish. Those who were actually there saw some magical performances that night.

The two teams combined for 1,025 yards of total offense, 552 from the Redskins and 473 from Green Bay.

Washington quarterback Joe Theismann blistered Green Bay's secondary, completing 27 of 39 passes for 398 yards and two touchdowns.

TOP TEN

Most Consecutive Games Rushing for Touchdowns

1.	7	Paul Hornung	1960
2.	6	Terdell Middleton	1978
3.	5t	Tobin Rote	1956
	5t	Jim Taylor (twice)	1961, 1964
	5t	Brent Fullwood	1988
	5t	Ahman Green	2003–2004
7.	4t	Verne Lewellen (three times)	1929, 1929–1930, 1931
	4t	Charlie Sample	1942
	4t	Jim Taylor (three times)	1961, 1962 (twice)
	4t	Donny Anderson	1971

But Dickey matched him throw for throw, hitting on 22 of 30 for 387 yards and three TDs.

"It was a cool night, and it was just one of those nights where the ball was just spinning out of my hand," Dickey said. "I couldn't have thrown a wobbly pass if I tried.

"That first half, [tight end] Paul Coffman and I were just playing catch. He came back to the huddle one time and I said, 'Can you believe how easy this is?'"

Coffman certainly made it look easy. The Packers' Pro Bowl tight end caught six passes for 124 yards and a pair of touchdowns.

"I remember getting home after that game and friends of mine from around the league had left messages like, 'You're going back to the Pro Bowl,'" Coffman recalled. "That was a great game. That's one people will never forget."

Green Bay's offensive line certainly won't forget it. The Packers front dominated a Washington defensive line that had wreaked havoc all year long.

Redskins defensive end Dexter Manley was as vocal as Warren leading up to the game, talking smack about

TRIVIA

Within ten thousand, how many stockholders do the Green Bay Packers have?

Answers to the trivia questions are on pages 162–163

By the NUMBERS

33—Paul Hornung had the most points ever in a game for Green Bay when he scored 33 points on four touchdowns, six extra points, and a field goal against the Baltimore Colts on October 8, 1961. Don Hutson scored 31 points in a 1945 game against Detroit, while Hornung also had games in which he scored 30 and 28 points.

the havoc *he* planned to cause. Instead, Green Bay left tackle Karl Swanke muted Manley, and the Packers controlled the line of scrimmage, allowing their offense to be louder than ever.

"Dexter had kind of spouted off in the papers before that game that he was going to wreak havoc," Swanke remembered. "Well, there were no disruptions with Lynn. That night was a culmination for [offensive coordinator] Bob Schnelker and our offense. Everything he called worked to perfection. It was an incredible night."

As great as it was for the offense, though, it was equally awful for the defense, and in the final moments, the Packers defense almost blew it.

Green Bay had taken its 48–47 lead after a 20-yard Jan Stenerud field goal. But the Packers left Theismann and the Redskins 54 seconds with which to work.

Washington quickly marched deep into Green Bay territory, and with just three seconds left, Redskins kicker Mark Moseley, the reigning NFL MVP who was four for four that night, lined up for a game-winning 39-yarder.

"I walked over to Jan, and I said, 'Do you believe this?'" Dickey said. "'We're going to lose this game. What a shame.'"

It didn't happen that way, though. Moseley, whom Dickey once held for in Houston, pushed his kick no more than a yard to the right. And while the Packers went on to a rather uneventful 8–8 season, that game was one they'll remember forever.

"That was as exciting a game as you'd ever want to be in," Dickey said. "National TV. A game decided in the last seconds. It's one I'll never forget."

Forrest Grump

What would happen if you threw a party and no one came?

Chances are Forrest Gregg would find out if his guest list consisted of players he once coached in Green Bay.

Gregg coached the Packers from 1984 to 1987, compiling a 25–37–1 record. And it's safe to say there weren't a lot of broken hearts when he resigned after four years.

"Forrest tried to be like [Vince] Lombardi, but he was no Lombardi," said Lew Carpenter, an assistant coach in Green Bay under both Bart Starr and Gregg. "Personally, I think he's a [expletive] head. You are what you are. You can't change that. And he's a [expletive] head."

"He ran down the football team in the media," said Greg Koch, a Packers tackle from 1977 to 1985. "Then, if you do well, it's the coach who looks good. But the truth is he was not a good football coach."

The evidence certainly supports Koch's claim.

Gregg had been a brilliant right tackle during the Packers' Glory Years. He was named to nine Pro Bowls and was an eight-time All-Pro selection. In fact, Lombardi once called him the "finest player I ever coached."

Gregg was Cleveland's head coach for three years and coached Cincinnati for four seasons, leading the Bengals to a Super Bowl appearance. When Green Bay fired Bart Starr after nine seasons in 1983, the organization thought it hit the jackpot with Gregg.

Instead, the Packers got a lemon.

Gregg's people skills were laughable. He thought driving his team hard all week would toughen them up for Sunday's game, when instead it simply wore them out. And he created a divided locker room by making no secret he was weeding out Starr's players.

Forrest Gregg starred on the Packers' offensive line during their glory years under Vince Lombardi, but he was no Lombardi himself as the team's head coach. Photo courtesy of Vernon Biever.

"Bart and Forrest were like night and day," former Packers quarterback Lynn Dickey said. "Bart would work you extremely hard physically. I've never worked harder than I did under Bart. But he treated people with decency and treated you like a man.

"Forrest came in and he yelled at you, and he insulted you in front of the team. Some things went on with him that would never work at any level.

"I remember our first meeting with Forrest. He was berating guys he didn't even know. He said, 'Some of you guys have been living on easy street. Like you, McCarren.' Well, Larry McCarren was probably the hardest-working guy on the team, making about $220,000 a year.

"Forrest knew his X's and O's, but he had no idea about people skills. And he brought in his own guys, and they walked all over him. They were late for meetings, and Forrest would say, 'If that happens again you'll be out of here.' Well, by the 10th week of the year, it was the same idle threats. They knew they weren't going anywhere. It was a bad situation."

The Packers went 8–8 in each of Gregg's first two years. Then before the 1986 season, he decided to clean house.

Gregg cut several veterans, including Dickey and 30-year-old tight end Paul Coffman, who had reached the Pro Bowl in 1984. He then made the mistake of going with youthful players he had hand-picked who either weren't ready or simply weren't good enough.

The result? Green Bay went 4–12 in 1986 and 5–9–1 the following season.

TRIVIA

Against which team did Green Bay earn its first-ever win?

A. Chicago Cardinals
B. Rock Island Independents
C. Minneapolis Marines
D. Columbus Panhandlers

Answers to the trivia questions are on pages 162–163

"Forrest yelled a lot, and he cut some players who were pretty darn good," said Alphonso Carreker, a Packers defensive end from 1984 to 1988. "But that was Forrest's way. If he didn't like you, he cut you. Forrest wanted to be the Bobby Knight of football, and it's hard to motivate people that way. So I never paid Forrest any attention."

Adding insult to injury, Gregg's teams began to play like thugs. His final two teams remain the most penalized in franchise history. And the Charles Martin saga, in which the Packers defensive lineman ended Chicago quarterback Jim McMahon's 1986 season with a cheap shot, was an embarrassment for the once-proud organization.

There was once a time when a Packers ticket was among the toughest in sports for fans to get their hands on. Now, with Gregg in charge, people couldn't give them away.

"Forrest, he's someone I have nothing to say about," Coffman said.

"Bart was an exceptional person, someone I really enjoyed," said Mike Douglass, a Packers linebacker from 1978 to 1985. "I really respected how he went about things, and I thought we were getting to the point where we could start having some success. So when they fired him, I didn't approve of it. Then along comes Forrest Gregg, and he destroys the whole team. If you played for Bart, Forrest didn't want you. He killed a team that was on the rise."

IF ONLY . . . Dan Devine hadn't traded away five draft picks for over-the-hill quarterback John Hadl in 1974. Had Devine not made that dreadful decision, Bart Starr would have had more draft choices to work with and a better chance to succeed.

1,054—Ryan Longwell holds the franchise record for most career points. In his nine years with the Packers (1997–2005), Longwell made 226 field goals and 376 extra points. Receiver/kicker Don Hutson is second in all-time scoring with 823 points, and kicker Chris Jacke is third with 820.

As bad as things were on the field, they were even worse off it. Green Bay's players were showing up in the police report almost as often as they were in the sports pages. The Packers, once a great source of pride throughout the state, were now the butt of jokes everywhere.

"Forrest thought he knew it all," said Kenneth Davis, a Packers running back from 1986 to 1988. "He couldn't learn from anybody else."

By the end of the 1987 season, Gregg had learned he was working on borrowed time. When Southern Methodist University, his alma mater, asked him to try to resuscitate a program that had just received the death penalty, he jumped at it.

"I remember a reporter asked me what I thought about it," said Koch, who was playing in Minnesota at the time. "I said, 'He's the perfect guy for the program.' The reporter said, 'There isn't a program.' And I said, 'Exactly.'"

That general distaste seems to sum up the Gregg era.

"I don't think Forrest was right to come back to Green Bay," Carreker said. "He thought he could be the type of coach who would put you through punishing practices all year long and threaten you with words and that would make you a champion. But he didn't do anything that came close to making us champions. Those years were a disaster."

The Hit Man Goes Too Far

The Boston Red Sox have the New York Yankees. Alabama has Auburn, and Duke has North Carolina.

But you'd be hard-pressed to find a rivalry in sports that has been more heated through the years than the Green Bay Packers and the Chicago Bears. In 1986, though, the Packers crossed the line from intense to dirty.

During Green Bay's 4–12 season that year, Forrest Gregg's squad was incapable of hurting teams with its play. Harming them with cheap shots was another story.

Defensive lineman Charles Martin was at the center of one of the dirtiest plays you'll ever see.

In the second quarter of a November game at Chicago that year, Bears quarterback Jim McMahon threw an interception to Green Bay's Mark Lee. McMahon was trying to get out of the way when Martin raced toward him, grabbed him from behind, and put him in a bear hug. Martin then slammed McMahon to the turf on his already injured throwing shoulder.

Martin was immediately ejected for the flagrant late hit and was later suspended two games. McMahon missed the rest of the season, and the Bears' hopes of repeating as Super Bowl champions vanished.

"Ridiculous," Chicago coach Mike Ditka said of the play afterward. "I have nothing to do with Charles Martin, and hopefully I never will. They got some players that are really questionable."

"That was cheap, and there is no room for that sort of thing in football," said Bears safety Dave Duerson. "In the four years I've been here, I've only seen one hit that cheap. And that was also by a Packer."

Seven—Number of Packers who have rushed for at least 1,000 yards in a season. The list includes Tony Canadeo (1949), Jim Taylor (1960–1964), John Brockington (1971–1973), Terdell Middleton (1978), Edgar Bennett (1995), Dorsey Levens (1997, 1999), and Ahman Green (2000–2004).

Duerson was referring to Ken Stills' 1985 late hit on Bears fullback Matt Suhey. But Martin's was worse.

Martin and some of his defensive teammates wore "Terrible Towels" that day, with the numbers of various Chicago players on them. At the top of Martin's towel was McMahon's No. 9. And really, the only thing that was terrible was Martin's boorish behavior.

"All I know is somebody grabbed me from behind and threw me down," McMahon said. "You can tell it was a blatant thing to do."

Gregg's teams at that time lacked discipline, style, and character—setting team records for penalties. So it was no surprise they were celebrating Martin's thuggery on the sideline after it happened, then defending it after the game.

"That's the name of the game," Packers defensive back Mossy Cade said. "Football is an aggressive sport. If Chicago doesn't like it, they have to live with it."

The Packers tried selling the idea that because McMahon had just thrown an interception, Martin was simply trying to dispose of the punky QB. But Martin never made an effort to block McMahon—unless WWF moves constituted blocking under Gregg's watch.

"We're taught anytime we get an interception, you go after the first thing you see, preferably the quarterback," said Martin, who died of renal disease in January 2005. "I got a little too rough. They [the Bears] can do it to you, but you can't do it to them."

"We tell people if we intercept a pass, go get anybody near you," Green Bay defensive coordinator Dick Modzelewski said. "It's OK if you go after a guy and over him and rough him up a little bit. But to pick him up and

TRIVIA

Green Bay has 21 players in the Pro Football Hall of Fame, second most in the NFL. Who's first?

Answers to the trivia questions are on pages 162–163

throw him down—the way they protect quarterbacks now, you can't even brush his pants off for him."

Excuses and rationalizations were commonplace during Gregg's forgettable stint as coach. But there was no defense for this.

It was one of the uglier moments in team history.

An Instant Classic

There are those breathtaking moments, those spine-tingling, hair-raising times that sports fans never forget. Not only is a play, a game, an event etched in their minds, everything about it still seems as if it took place yesterday.

Ask Green Bay Packers fans where they were, who they were with, even what they were wearing on November 5, 1989, and chances are they'll know.

It was that day when Packers quarterback Don Majkowski became a legend, Green Bay slew its archrival, and the words instant replay captivated the state of Wisconsin.

The Packers trailed Chicago, 13–7, that day with just 41 seconds left in the game and faced a fourth-and-goal from the Bears' 14-yard line. Majkowski dropped to pass, then was forced out of the pocket and scrambled to his right.

Majkowski got perilously close to the line of scrimmage, then fired back across his body and hit Sterling Sharpe with a 14-yard TD pass. But line judge Jim Quirk ruled Majkowski had crossed the line of scrimmage and took away the touchdown and an apparent Green Bay victory.

The call went to the instant replay booth, and after a delay of nearly five minutes, the ruling on the field was reversed and the touchdown stood.

Green Bay 14, Chicago 13.

The Lambeau Field crowd of 55,566 went crazy. And the entire state followed suit.

"People, wherever I go, if I'm traveling back to Wisconsin or around the United States, Packers fans come up to me and that's the first thing

Don Majkowski beat the rival Bears with his last-minute touchdown toss in the now infamous Instant Replay Game. Photo courtesy of Getty Images.

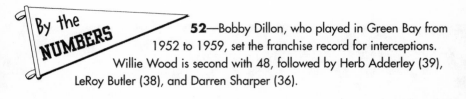

and the only thing they want to talk about," Majkowski said. "And they always seem to tell me the same story. They always say, 'I remember exactly where I was watching that game.' It had a huge impact on people. And that's pretty unique."

In the eighties it had become unique for the Packers to defeat the Bears. Chicago had won eight straight games against Green Bay—its longest streak in a series that dates back to 1921. Packers fans were desperate for a win over the hated Bears, and the drama that surrounded the victory made it even sweeter.

"That's probably my defining moment as a Green Bay Packer, my most famous play," Majkowski said. "And I'm proud to be remembered from that game. That game had such significant meaning to the Packers fans because the Bears of the mideighties and late eighties were so dominant. And to finally end the streak at home on the last play of the game in such dramatic fashion is pretty memorable. And to this day, that game goes down as one of the five most memorable games in Lambeau Field."

That's for sure. And not just because of the result, but also because of the almost surreal wait before the call was reversed.

Replay official Bill Parkinson said the deciding factor in his call was where the ball was released, not where Majkowski's feet were.

"On stop and start on the instant replay, the initial line feed showed that the ball did not cross the line of scrimmage, the 14-yard line," Parkinson told reporters afterward. "This was a very important play. The ballgame hinges on this play. We took our time and looked at both feeds."

TRIVIA

Through 2005, Green Bay played 38 postseason games. What is the Packers' won-loss record?

Answers to the trivia questions are on pages 162–163

The Bears have never agreed with either feed. Chicago bemoaned the ruling afterward. And to this day, the Bears media guide has an asterisk next to that game.

"I've seen [Chicago coach Mike] Ditka after the fact, and he still won't admit that I was behind the line," Majkowski said. "They couldn't even admit they lost that game fair and square. It's kind of like they're still crying about it. It just shows how much the Bears couldn't stand to have lost that game. It hurt 'em. And that just makes it that much sweeter."

Tony Mandarich: The Incredible Bust

Ryan Leaf. Brian Bosworth. Aundray Bruce. Tim Couch. Akili Smith.

These names most certainly come up when discussing the NFL's worst draft picks over the past 20 years. But no discussion is complete without mentioning Tony Mandarich.

Green Bay took Mandarich with the second pick in the 1989 draft. And the massive offensive lineman from Michigan State was such a flop, he undoubtedly ranks as the worst pick in Packers history.

Green Bay has had some other colossal misses, such as Rich Campbell (6th in 1981), Jamal Reynolds (10th in 2001), and Brent Fullwood (4th in 1987). But Mandarich is in a league of his own when it comes to disappointment.

"When I'm called one of the biggest busts ever, I know it's the truth," said Mandarich, who's currently the general manager of a golf course in Ontario, Canada. "The truth is the truth. It's nothing I don't already know."

Heading into the 1989 draft, the hype machine was cranked to high regarding Mandarich. He was widely regarded as the best offensive line prospect ever after measuring 6'5", 315 pounds and running a 4.65 40-yard dash at the NFL scouting combine that year. Many believed the league had never seen a left tackle with such speed, and at that time, Mandarich outweighed the other top tackles by a good 25 pounds.

Mandarich could bench-press more than 500 pounds. He ate seven meals and fifteen thousand calories a day. The term "pancake block" was created specifically for his exploits at Michigan State. He trained with Mr. America Rory Leidelmeyer. And he seemed as sure of a sure thing as you'd ever find, at least according to those doing the drafting.

Ernie Accorsi, then the vice president of football operations for the Cleveland Browns, said, "He is perfect."

By the NUMBERS

14—Green Bay's longest streak without a losing season came from 1934 to 1947. The Packers also went 13 years without a losing season between 1992 and 2004 and 12 years from 1921 to 1932.

The late John Butler, then the college scouting director for the Buffalo Bills, said, "Mandarich is in a class by himself. He wears an S on his chest."

Only if that S stood for Superbust.

"Tony was a product of his environment," said Ron Hallstrom, the Packers' right guard during the Mandarich era. "He was the prototypical guy who knew how to sell a contract. It was the Brian Bosworth effect."

In three years on the field and one on injured reserve, Mandarich gave the Packers virtually nothing for their four-year, $4.4 million investment. To this day, Mandarich knows exactly why.

"My problems had nothing at all to do with Green Bay," he said. "They had everything to do with me. I had a bad attitude; I was arrogant and extremely cocky and thought I knew everything. I look back at the situation and I was lucky to go to a place like Green Bay with great fans and all that tradition. And I shot myself in the foot."

Mandarich says he's a different person today, someone who learned a lot of lessons from past mistakes. And he certainly made plenty of mistakes while in Green Bay.

Mandarich said from the day he was drafted that he didn't want to play in Green Bay, even though he had never stepped foot in the city. He skipped minicamp and didn't sign with the Packers until two days before the season opener.

"The lessons I've learned are priceless," Mandarich said. "And the person I am today, that's a good thing. But obviously I would change things if I could. Looking back, I would have loved to be in Green Bay 15 years and contribute instead of being part of the problem."

Getting Mandarich signed was only the Packers' first problem. Their biggest issue came when they realized he couldn't play.

TRIVIA

Green Bay has 12 NFL championships. How many franchises have more?

Answers to the trivia questions are on pages 162–163

TOP TEN Highest Passer Rating in a Season

1.	105.0	Bart Starr	1966
2.	99.5	Brett Favre	1995
3.	97.1	Bart Starr	1964
4.	95.8	Brett Favre	1996
5.	94.1	Brett Favre	2001
6.	92.6	Brett Favre	1997
7.	92.4	Brett Favre	2004
8.	90.7†	Bart Starr	1962
	90.7†	Brett Favre	1994
10.	90.4	Brett Favre	2003

Mandarich made his reputation as a devastating run blocker at Michigan State, where the Spartans ran the ball the overwhelming majority of the time. Green Bay, however, threw the ball roughly 60 percent of the time, and Mandarich wasn't close to being up to speed as a pass blocker.

Mandarich backed up left tackle Alan Veingrad as a rookie and played in just nine series. Then, in 1990, he started 16 games and led the team in sacks allowed (12½), quarterback knockdowns allowed (22½), and penalties (8).

His play improved somewhat when he started 15 games at right tackle in 1991, but he still led the team in sacks allowed (8½) and quarterback knockdowns allowed (13½). Then the Packers traded for Tootie Robbins in February 1992 and tried Mandarich at both left guard and left tackle.

But Mandarich never suited up in 1992 after suffering a severe concussion that preseason that left him with postconcussion syndrome. Mandarich was also being treated for a thyroid condition.

That off-season, the Packers chose not to spend the $660,000 it would take to maintain his rights. And the miserable Mandarich years were over.

"At the end of my four years, I felt it was the Packers' fault and the media's fault, but it wasn't my fault," Mandarich said. "Then you get away from it for a year or so and you realize that you didn't have it so bad. Now

I know that the whole thing was my fault, and a lot of that comes with age and maturity."

Mandarich was widely suspected of using steroids at Michigan State. And when *The Detroit News* investigated the Spartans' program in 1990, Mandarich's name came up in almost all of the 100 interviews the paper did.

Former teammate Jeff Case told the paper that Mandarich injected him with testosterone seven to eight times a day and that vials of drugs lined Mandarich's kitchen cabinet.

The general belief throughout the NFL was Mandarich beat the NCAA-administered tests but got off the drug once he reached the NFL because he didn't want to face the heavier penalties. Mandarich, though, insists he never used steroids.

"Absolutely never," said Mandarich, who says he only used multivitamins and creatine. "You'll have guys who disagree with that. I mean everyone is entitled to their own opinions. But I never did them."

Regardless, he was probably the most overhyped player in Packers history. And even though Mandarich doesn't spend much time wondering "what if?" he does admit he wished things could have been much, much different.

"I don't really sit around and lament what Packers fans think about me," he said. "I'm not trying to win the fans back or anything like that. I would just say I made a lot of mistakes, and I was extremely lucky to learn from those mistakes.

"I should have just kept my mouth shut and not been so arrogant and talked so much [expletive]. I should have eliminated that from my game. And me being a guy that had a big mouth, I don't like that anymore.

"Take a guy like T.O. [Terrell Owens]. He does it, but he backs it up and then it's not ridiculous. I think you can do it if you back it up. But when you had a guy like me doing it who didn't back it up, then it's a lot more ridiculous. But what can I say, I'm human and I made a lot of mistakes."

But none as big as the one Green Bay made in drafting him.

By the NUMBERS **19**—Fee Klaus, a center in 1921, is the youngest player in Packers history.

"I Got the Guy": Wolf Lands Favre

The phone calls dragged on for more than two months. Three or four times a week, Green Bay general manager Ron Wolf and Atlanta's vice president of player personnel Ken Herock would exchange calls. And the two would bicker back and forth about the details involving a young man who had never completed a pass in the National Football League—quarterback Brett Favre.

"It was a long process, and it took a very long time," Wolf said during a 2005 interview from his home in Annapolis, Maryland. "It took a lot of phone calls. It was constant posturing."

In retrospect, it was worth every bit of effort—for Wolf, that is.

Wolf eventually gave up a first-round pick for Favre, a player who was taken in the second round of the 1991 draft. The Packers' GM took plenty of heat for it at the time.

But history will show that trade was the best in Packers history. And Wolf, who cemented his place among the greatest general managers ever when he made the deal, argues the trade ranks among the best in NFL history.

"I don't know what people say is the best trade ever made," Wolf said. "But I've got to use the words here of Bum Phillips, and he said this about Earl Campbell: 'I don't know if he's the best, but it won't take long to call the roll.' And that's kind of the way I feel about this. If it's not the best, it won't take long to call the roll."

Wolf fell in love with Favre when he was heading the New York Jets scouting department. Wolf had every intention of using the Jets' second-round pick in 1991—the 33rd overall selection—on Favre that year. But one pick before Wolf was set to select, the Falcons took Favre and Wolf settled on Browning Nagle.

In November of that same year, Wolf was hired by Green Bay and given total control of its football operations. Ironically, the Packers' first game after Wolf's hiring was at Atlanta, where Favre was a third stringer who had fallen out of favor with coach Jerry Glanville and management because of his carefree approach to the game.

"Ron came by about an hour before the game, put his briefcase down on the chair next to me, and said, 'I'm going to go down on the field and look at Atlanta's backup quarterback. If his arm is still as strong as it was coming out of college, we're going to go after him,'" said Bob Harlan, who has been Green Bay's president since 1989. "So Ron left and I started looking at the roster to see who the backup quarterback [was]. And Ron came back shortly before kickoff and said, 'Bob, we're going to make a trade for Brett Favre. Are you OK with that?' And I told

Acquiring Brett Favre from Atlanta, as Packers general manager Ron Wolf did, rates as one of the best deals in league history.

GOOD THING . . . Green Bay hired Ron Wolf as its general manager in 1991. Had the Packers hired someone else, it's unlikely that person would have felt as strongly about quarterback Brett Favre as Wolf did. And it's even more unlikely that anyone other than Wolf would have given up a first-round draft choice to bring Favre to Green Bay.

him, 'I promised you it was your team to run, there would be no interference. I'm fine with it.'"

The challenge, of course, was getting the deal done. But Wolf knew all along that Herock, whom he had worked with in Oakland's front office during the seventies, was willing to deal.

"I knew that we could get him because really my first day on the job from a football standpoint, from a game standpoint, was the Atlanta game," Wolf recalled. "And I knew at that time I was going to be able to get him because Ken told me if I wanted to see how he threw I would have to watch him before the team came out. So I knew right then and there that I could get the guy.

"At that point, we came back and at some point we had an executive committee meeting. I told the people that we were going to make a commitment for this quarterback, told them all about this quarterback, Brett Favre, and how we were going to go to work to get him. They had no idea who I was talking about. But they were all for it."

So Wolf got right to work. For roughly the next 10 weeks, he and Herock talked at least every other day.

Wolf initially tried making the deal for a second-round pick. And when the Falcons wouldn't budge off a number one pick, Wolf tried getting a third rounder in return. The posturing went on for weeks, but never did Wolf feel the deal was close to being dead.

"I never had that feeling," Wolf said. "Because I knew that they wanted to get rid of him. It was just a matter of getting it done. I knew we were going to get this deal done because I didn't think anyone was going to pay what they were asking other than me. Finally the call came that said, 'It's got to be a first or we're not going to make the trade.'"

Even though it defied logic to many—giving up a first-round pick for a former second rounder who had career statistics of zero for four with two interceptions—Wolf pulled the trigger. On February 10, 1992, he traded the 17th overall pick in the 1992 draft for Favre.

"I started hearing from a lot of angry fans, and they were very upset," Harlan said. "And the newspapers were questioning the move and so forth. But you know, Ron was convinced. And giving up a number one for someone that wasn't a major player at that time,

TRIVIA

True or false: Green Bay was the first team ever to fly to a road game.

Answers to the trivia questions are on pages 162–163

you wonder. But I tell you what, I had great confidence in Ron Wolf. And his mind was made up. He went after Brett, and thank God he did."

Although Wolf was taking a beating publicly at the time, he didn't care. It was his ability to disregard public perception that helped to make him so good at what he did.

"I didn't care at all, because I got the guy," Wolf said of the heat he took. "In my mind, that guy was a Hall of Fame player and he was going to turn the fortunes of the franchise completely around. And he did all those things."

Did he ever.

Favre is the only player in league history to win three Most Valuable Player awards. He led Green Bay to a Super Bowl championship in 1996. In Favre's first 14 years as Green Bay's quarterback, the Packers had just one losing season. And heading into 2006, Favre is in position to break many of Dan Marino's hallowed passing records.

"I was very confident," Wolf said. "I gave up a number one. He was drafted in the second round, wasn't good enough to play for them. But I was very confident he was going to be the guy.

"I looked at it like this: if I was going to be successful, I was going to be successful because of Brett Favre. And if he wasn't good enough, then I wasn't going to be successful. So I put everything on him, and it worked out."

By the NUMBERS

176—Paul Hornung set the team record for points in a season. In 1960 Hornung had 15 touchdowns, 41 extra points, and 15 field goals. Hornung is also second on this list, scoring 146 points in 1961, while Don Hutson is third with 138 points in 1942.

The Start of Something Wonderful

September 20, 1992, seemed like just another day when Brett Favre rolled out of bed.

Favre drove over to Lambeau Field for his third game as a Green Bay Packer. He expected to spend his day watching Don Majkowski quarterback the team, and maybe Favre would get in for some mop-up duty in Green Bay's game with Cincinnati.

Instead, that day was nothing like anyone could have expected.

On that day, the fortunes of a downtrodden franchise changed for good. On that day, an organization that had become loveable losers found hope. On that day, Brett Favre had his coming-out party.

"I'll never forget that day," Packers president Bob Harlan said.

Nor should he.

On that gorgeous autumn afternoon, Favre replaced an injured Majkowski and engineered one of the greatest comebacks in team history. In the final four minutes of the game, Favre led scoring drives of 88 and 92 yards as Green Bay rallied past Cincinnati, 24–23, for coach Mike Holmgren's first NFL victory. Favre capped the dramatics with a 35-yard bullet score to Kitrick Taylor with just 13 seconds left.

Since that unforgettable day, Favre has won three Most Valuable Player awards, led the Packers to the 1996 Super Bowl title, and has had just one losing season in 14 years as Green Bay's starting quarterback. Favre has started 221 consecutive games, nearly doubling the old mark held by Ron Jaworski (116), and he is waging an assault on almost every passing record there is.

"I shudder to think where we would have been without him," said former Green Bay general manager Ron Wolf, who had traded for Favre in early 1992. "Without a doubt in my mind, he's the player of the nineties."

But back on September 20, 1992, Favre was nothing but a mystery to most.

"If there's anything I remember about that day, it was just like, 'Wow! Where did this guy come from?'" said former Green Bay linebacker Brian Noble, a teammate of Favre's in 1992–1993. "I hadn't seen much of him in training camp, and all I knew was he was a young kid with a little bit of baggage. But after that day, people knew about Brett."

Did they ever.

Until then, all people knew about Favre was that former Atlanta head coach Jerry Glanville wanted him out of town after Favre's rookie season with the Falcons was more about bar-hopping and carousing than it was about football. Wolf, who desperately wanted to select Favre in the 1991 draft when he was with the New York Jets, was happy to oblige.

On February 10, 1992, Wolf sent a number one draft choice to Atlanta for a player who had career passing statistics of zero completions in four attempts and two interceptions. Although critics balked at the move then, they'd likely agree with Wolf today that acquiring Favre was one of the five most lopsided trades in NFL history.

"I knew right away we had something special," Wolf said. "The question was, how were we going to get him to play? You could tell it was just a matter of time as soon as training camp started. And during camp, Holmgren and I had a long talk about how to get him on the field."

Turns out, their dilemma took care of itself. With the Packers coming off a 31–3 loss in Tampa Bay in week 2, Holmgren had contemplated making a quarterback switch before the Cincinnati game. But Holmgren stuck with Majkowski as his starter, fearing Favre wasn't quite ready.

On Green Bay's second series of the game, however, Majkowski was sacked by Bengals defensive tackle Tim Krumrie and suffered ligament damage to his left ankle. As he was being helped off the field, NBC announcer Jim Lampley asked, "Will it ever be 1989 for the Majik Man, Don Majkowski, again? It does not appear likely."

TRIVIA

Brett Favre completed a two-point-conversion pass in Super Bowl XXXI. Who caught it?

Answers to the trivia questions are on pages 162–163

TOP TEN

Most Yards Passing in a Season

1.	4,458	Lynn Dickey	1983
2.	4,413	Brett Favre	1995
3.	4,318	Don Majkowski	1989
4.	4,212	Brett Favre	1998
5.	4,091	Brett Favre	1999
6.	4,088	Brett Favre	2004
7.	3,921	Brett Favre	2001
8.	3,899	Brett Favre	1996
9.	3,882	Brett Favre	1994
10.	3,881	Brett Favre	2005

Little did Lampley know how prophetic those words would be. And little did people know the type of magic Favre would begin creating.

The early returns in the Cincinnati game certainly weren't encouraging. It was apparent that Favre and the number one offense hadn't spent a lot of time together. On his 11th play from scrimmage, Favre fumbled a snap from center James Campen, and Krumrie recovered for Cincinnati.

Favre's overeagerness was evident as he overshot wide-open receivers Sterling Sharpe and Sanjay Beach in the second quarter. And Favre's frustration was beginning to build after he fumbled on back-to-back plays late in the third quarter.

"It's been so long, but I can tell you this: when I became a starter, I had no clue what was going on," Favre said during a 2002 interview. "Maybe that was good. If I told you [back then] I knew what was going on, I was feeding you a line of BS."

Green Bay headed to the fourth quarter trailing 17–3, and had not scored a touchdown in seven quarters.

But the light seemed to go on for Favre and the entire offense in the fourth quarter. Terrell Buckley, playing his first game as a Packer, gave the team a jump start when he returned a punt 58 yards for a touchdown with 12:43 remaining to trim the Bengals' lead to 17–10.

After a Jim Breech field goal gave Cincinnati a 20–10 advantage, Green Bay started at its own 12. And Favre began to look like he had been playing in Holmgren's West Coast offense for years, not weeks.

Favre guided an eight-play, 88-yard drive in which he made a handful of standout plays. On a third-and-six, he eluded the rush and ran for 19 yards. He then fired a 15-yard completion to Harry Sydney and lofted a gorgeous 33-yarder to a wide-open Sharpe, bringing Green Bay to the Bengals' 17.

After a 10-yard bullet to Ed West and an Edgar Bennett run, Favre found Sharpe for a five-yard score over the middle to bring the score to 20–17. The touchdown pass was the first of Favre's career and would be the first of 41 on which he and Sharpe would connect.

"We knew he was going to be a good player just from watching him in training camp," running back Vince Workman said of Favre. "Most of his passes were just rocket passes. You noticed his arm strength right away, especially because Majkowski was more of a finesse passer. But he [Favre] stepped in that day and took control right away. He had the respect of everybody right away."

If he didn't then, he certainly did by the time the game ended.

Another Breech field goal for Cincinnati with 1:07 left made it 23–17. Then rookie wide receiver Robert Brooks dug the Packers an even bigger hole when he caught the ensuing kickoff on the left sideline and stepped out of bounds at the 8.

All Favre needed to do now was lead Green Bay 92 yards in 1:07 without the benefit of a timeout. No problem, right?

"Brett had a swagger to him, even back then," said left tackle Ken Ruettgers, who played with Favre through the 1996 season. "Even though he was 23 or whatever, it was like nothing could phase him."

And the improbable odds certainly didn't slow him down on this day.

On first down, Favre couldn't find an open man and settled on a swing pass to Sydney, who was smart enough to run out of bounds after gaining four yards. On second down, Favre stepped up into the pocket to avoid the rush, then found Sharpe wide open down the right sideline.

Sharpe had run past cornerback Rod Jones, and help was late arriving from safety Fernandus Vinson. Sharpe reached up high to haul in the 41-yard bullet from Favre, but in doing so, reaggravated a rib injury.

With the clock running, Favre raced to the line of scrimmage, then dumped a 12-yard completion to Vince Workman over the middle to

29—Don Hutson once scored 29 points in a single quarter, which is still an NFL record. Hutson had four touchdowns and five extra points in the second quarter of a game against Detroit in 1945.

bring the Packers to the Bengals' 35. Again, Favre raced to the line and spiked the ball with just 19 ticks remaining.

With Sharpe having gone to the sideline because of his rib injury, things looked dicey for Green Bay. The Packers lined up with Brooks in the slot on the left, Beach wide left, and Taylor wide right. Favre again looked right, where just three plays earlier he had found a wide-open Sharpe.

Favre pump-faked in Taylor's direction and got Jones to bite. Taylor streaked by Jones and had a good three yards of separation. Favre then fired a laser beam to Taylor that didn't get more than 12 feet off the ground. It was a good thing, too. Vinson was closing fast, and had there been more air under the ball, the Bengals safety would have likely broken up the pass.

Instead, Favre's bullet threaded the needle between the two Cincinnati defenders and landed right on Taylor's hands with 13 seconds remaining.

The memorable touchdown pass would be the only one on which Favre and Taylor would ever connect.

"On that play, I was blocking on a guy and he just kind of stopped," Ruettgers said. "That usually means he's given up because the ball is in the air. So I looked up and saw the ball just zipping down the field to Kitrick Taylor. I mean, it was an NFL Films moment. It was one of the few great moments that as a lineman you not only played but got to witness at the same time. It was incredible."

In typical Favre fashion, he showed his boyish enthusiasm, ripping off his helmet and dancing around Lambeau Field. The rest of the Packers and the sellout crowd went ballistic as well.

"I was standing on about the 40 when he threw it," Noble said. "And I remember thinking, 'I'm glad I'm not on the field, because that ball would have hit me in the head.' There was no elevation to it. It was an incredible throw."

"I'm just really proud to say I was part of that game and proud to say I played with Brett when he was starting out," said Workman, who was Green Bay's leading rusher that game. "That day and that play really gave us an extra boost of confidence. It was our first victory, and it helped us start to believe in ourselves."

That it did. Favre would lead Green Bay on a six-game winning streak later that year and to a 9–7 record for just its second winning season since 1982.

More than that, though, Favre showed the poise, leadership, and ability that have made him one of the greatest to ever play the position.

"He's come a long way," said former Packers center Frank Winters. "What he's accomplished in this league speaks for itself. There's no need to really dwell on it. What he has accomplished is amazing, and the guy's probably a shoo-in for the Hall of Fame."

Added Ruettgers, "It's been an honor to watch him mature as a player and a person. And to say I played with one of the all-time greats will be a pretty special thing."

What is just as special is how the fame, fortune, and notoriety have had virtually no impact on Favre. He's still the same down-to-earth, country bumpkin from Kiln, Mississippi, that he's always been and will likely always be.

"From my standpoint, I'm fairly simple," Favre said. "Much has been said about me in the off-season about me riding my tractor and cutting grass, but that's all I do. And aside from football, if I'm not on my property, I'm playing golf and playing with my kids.

"I feel fortunate that from day one, I knew how fortunate I was to play and get paid to play football. I love to play the game and appreciate the opportunity."

Probably not as much as Packers fans have appreciated the opportunity to watch Favre since that magical day.

Quarterback Shuffle . . . Everywhere but Green Bay

Brett Favre started 221 consecutive games for the Green Bay Packers between September 27, 1992, and January 1, 2006. In that time, 21 of the NFL's remaining 31 franchises have had at least 10 starting quarterbacks. The Chicago Bears lead the way with 20 different starters in that time, and multiple other teams have started several quarterbacks as well.

Here's a look at each team and the various quarterbacks they've trotted out since Favre began his remarkable run.

Arizona/Phoenix (16): Steve Beuerlein, Jeff Blake, Dave Brown, Stoney Case, Chris Chandler, Boomer Esiason, Kent Graham, Shaun King, Dave Krieg, Josh McCown, Jim McMahon, John Navarre, Jake Plummer, Timm Rosenbach, Jay Schroeder, Kurt Warner

Atlanta (13): Chris Chandler, Steve DeBerg, Jeff George, Tony Graziani, Bobby Hebert, Doug Johnson, Danny Kanell, Kurt Kittner, Chris Miller, Matt Schaub, Billy Joe Tolliver, Michael Vick, Wade Wilson

Baltimore (13): Tony Banks, Jeff Blake, Kyle Boller, Stoney Case, Randall Cunningham, Trent Dilfer, Elvis Grbac, Jim Harbaugh, Scott Mitchell, Chris Redman, Vinny Testaverde, Anthony Wright, Eric Zeier

Buffalo (9): Drew Bledsoe, Todd Collins, Doug Flutie, Kelly Holcomb, Rob Johnson, Jim Kelly, J. P. Losman, Frank Reich, Alex Van Pelt

Carolina (8): Steve Beuerlein, Kerry Collins, Jake Delhomme, Randy Fasani, Matt Lytle, Rodney Peete, Frank Reich, Chris Weinke

Chicago (20): Henry Burris, Chris Chandler, Will Furrer, Rex Grossman, Jim Harbaugh, Chad Hutchinson, Erik Kramer, Craig Krenzel, Dave Krieg, Shane Matthews, Cade McNown, Jim Miller, Rick Mirer, Moses Moreno, Kyle Orton, Jonathan Quinn, Steve Stenstrom, Kordell Stewart, Steve Walsh, Peter Tom Willis

By the **NUMBERS**

223—Quarterback Brett Favre has played in more games than anyone else in franchise history. Bart Starr is second (196), while Ray Nitschke (190), Forrest Gregg (187), and LeRoy Butler (181) round out the top five.

Cincinnati (12): Jeff Blake, Boomer Esiason, Gus Frerotte, Donald Hollas, Paul Justin, Jon Kitna, David Klingler, Scott Mitchell, Neil O'Donnell, Carson Palmer, Jay Schroeder, Akili Smith

Cleveland (15): Tim Couch, Ty Detmer, Trent Dilfer, Charlie Frye, Jeff Garcia, Kelly Holcomb, Bernie Kosar, Luke McCown, Doug Pederson, Todd Philcox, Mark Rypien, Vinny Testaverde, Mike Tomczak, Spergon Wynn, Eric Zeier

Dallas (14): Troy Aikman, Drew Bledsoe, Quincy Carter, Randall Cunningham, Jason Garrett, Drew Henson, Chad Hutchinson, Bernie Kosar, Ryan Leaf, Rodney Peete, Clint Stoerner, Vinny Testaverde, Wade Wilson, Anthony Wright

Denver (12): Steve Beuerlein, Bubby Brister, John Elway, Gus Frerotte, Brian Griese, Jarious Jackson, Danny Kanell, Tommy Maddox, Hugh Millen, Chris Miller, Bill Musgrave, Jake Plummer

Detroit (14): Charlie Batch, Stoney Case, Ty Detmer, Gus Frerotte, Jeff Garcia, Joey Harrington, Erik Kramer, Dave Krieg, Don Majkowski, Mike McMahon, Scott Mitchell, Rodney Peete, Frank Reich, Andre Ware

Green Bay (1): Brett Favre

Houston (3): Tony Banks, David Carr, Dave Ragone

Indianapolis (10): Craig Erickson, Jeff George, Jim Harbaugh, Kelly Holcomb, Paul Justin, Don Majkowski, Peyton Manning, Browning Nagle, Jim Sorgi, Jack Trudeau

Jacksonville (9): Steve Beuerlein, Mark Brunell, Jay Fiedler, David Garrard, Rob Johnson, Byron Leftwich, Jamie Martin, Steve Matthews, Jonathan Quinn

Kansas City (7): Steve Bono, Rich Gannon, Elvis Grbac, Trent Green, Dave Krieg, Joe Montana, Warren Moon

Miami (12): Steve DeBerg, Craig Erickson, A. J. Feeley, Jay Fiedler, Gus Frerotte, Brian Griese, Damon Huard, Bernie Kosar, Ray Lucas, Dan Marino, Scott Mitchell, Sage Rosenfels

Brett Favre spends a minute with friend and Super Bowl XXXII opponent John Elway before the big game on January 25, 1998.

Minnesota (11): Todd Bouman, Dante Culpepper, Randall Cunningham, Gus Frerotte, Rich Gannon, Jeff George, Brad Johnson, Jim McMahon, Warren Moon, Sean Salisbury, Spergon Wynn

New England (7): Drew Bledsoe, Tom Brady, Jeff Carlson, Tom Hodson, Hugh Millen, Scott Secules, Scott Zolak

New Orleans (15): Jeff Blake, Todd Bouman, Aaron Brooks, Mike Buck, Kerry Collins, Jake Delhomme, Jim Everett, Bobby Hebert, Billy Joe

Hobert, Doug Nussmeier, Heath Shuler, Billy Joe Tolliver, Steve Walsh, Wade Wilson, Danny Wuerffel

New York Giants (9): Dave Brown, Kerry Collins, Kent Graham, Jeff Hostetler, Danny Kanell, Eli Manning, Jesse Palmer, Phil Simms, Kurt Warner

New York Jets (15): Brooks Bollinger, Bubby Brister, Quincy Carter, Boomer Esiason, Jay Fiedler, Glenn Foley, Ray Lucas, Rick Mirer, Browning Nagle, Ken O'Brien, Neil O'Donnell, Chad Pennington, Frank Reich, Vinny Testaverde, Jack Trudeau

Oakland/Los Angeles Raiders (12): Kerry Collins, Vince Evans, Rich Gannon, Jeff George, Billy Joe Hobert, Donald Hollas, Jeff Hostetler, Todd Marinovich, Rick Mirer, Jay Schroeder, Marques Tuiasosopo, Wade Wilson

Philadelphia (12): Bubby Brister, Randall Cunningham, Koy Detmer, Ty Detmer, A. J. Feeley, Bobby Hoying, Jim McMahon, Mike McMahon, Donovan McNabb, Ken O'Brien, Doug Pederson, Rodney Peete

Pittsburgh (9): Charlie Batch, Bubby Brister, Kent Graham, Tommy Maddox, Jim Miller, Neil O'Donnell, Ben Roethlisberger, Kordell Stewart, Mike Tomczak

St. Louis/Los Angeles Rams (14): Tony Banks, Steve Bono, Marc Bulger, Chris Chandler, Scott Covington, Jim Everett, Ryan Fitzpatrick, Trent Green, Jamie Martin, Chris Miller, T. J. Rubley, Mark Rypien, Steve Walsh, Kurt Warner

San Diego (12): Drew Brees, Jim Everett, Doug Flutie, John Friesz, Gale Gilbert, Jim Harbaugh, Stan Humphries, Erik Kramer, Ryan Leaf, Moses Moreno, Sean Salisbury, Craig Whelihan

San Francisco (9): Ty Detmer, Ken Dorsey, Jim Druckenmiller, Jeff Garcia, Elvis Grbac, Tim Rattay, Alex Smith, Steve Stenstrom, Steve Young

Seattle (11): Trent Dilfer, Glenn Foley, John Friesz, Stan Gelbaugh, Matt Hasselbeck, Brock Huard, Jon Kitna, Dan McGwire, Rick Mirer, Warren Moon, Kelly Stouffer

Tampa Bay (10): Steve DeBerg, Trent Dilfer, Craig Erickson, Brian

TRIVIA

Who holds the Packers' career record for interceptions?

Answers to the trivia questions are on pages 162–163

Griese, Brad Johnson, Rob Johnson, Shaun King, Chris Simms, Vinny Testaverde, Eric Zeier

Tennessee Titans/Houston Oilers (9): Cody Carlson, Chris Chandler, Will Furrer, Steve McNair, Warren Moon, Neil O'Donnell, Bucky Richardson, Billy Joe Tolliver, Billy Volek

Washington (16): Tony Banks, Mark Brunell, Cary Conklin, Gus Frerotte, John Friesz, Rich Gannon, Jeff George, Trent Green, Tim Hasselbeck, Jeff Hostetler, Brad Johnson, Shane Matthews, Patrick Ramsey, Mark Rypien, Heath Shuler, Danny Wuerffel

Favre by the Numbers

Brett Favre not only holds virtually every passing record in Green Bay history, but he's chasing several all-time marks as well. Here's a look at where Favre shapes up in several of history's most hallowed categories heading into the 2006 season.

Consecutive Starts, All-Time, by a Quarterback

221	Brett Favre, Green Bay	1992–present
128	Peyton Manning, Indianapolis	1998–present
116	Ron Jaworski, Philadelphia	1977–1984
107	Joe Ferguson, Buffalo	1977–1984
95	Dan Marino, Miami	1987–1993

Career Touchdown Passes

420	Dan Marino
396	Brett Favre
342	Fran Tarkenton
300	John Elway
291	Warren Moon

Career Passing Yards

Dan Marino	61,361
Brett Favre	53,615
John Elway	51,475
Warren Moon	49,325
Fran Tarkenton	47,003

Career Pass Completions

Dan Marino	4,967
Brett Favre	4,678
John Elway	4,123
Warren Moon	3,988
Fran Tarkenton	3,686

Career Passing Attempts

Dan Marino	8,358
Brett Favre	7,610
John Elway	7,250
Warren Moon	6,823
Fran Tarkenton	6,467

Overall Wins, Starting QB, All-Time

	W	L	T	Pct.
John Elway, Denver	148	82	1	.643
Dan Marino, Miami	147	93	0	.613
Brett Favre, Green Bay	139	82	0	.629
Fran Tarkenton, Minnesota/New York Giants	125	109	6	.533
Johnny Unitas, Baltimore/San Diego	119	63	4	.651

Best Home Record Since 1967

	W	L	Pct.
Terry Bradshaw, Pittsburgh	67	12	.848
Roger Staubach, Dallas	49	10	.831
John Elway, Denver	95	23	.805
Danny White, Dallas	37	10	.787
Brett Favre, Green Bay	86	24	.782

Other Favre Marks in Packers History (through the 2005 season)

7,606—Favre holds the franchise record for most pass attempts in his Green Bay career. Bart Starr is a distant second at 3,149.

45—Favre's number of 300-yard passing games.

61.50—Favre's all-time completion percentage ranks number one in Packers history. Starr ranks second at 57.42 percent.

86.0—Favre's career quarterback rating is the highest in team history. Starr is second (80.5), followed by Lynn Dickey (73.8) and Don Majkowski (73.5).

TRIVIA

Brett Favre and Antonio Freeman hooked up for more touchdowns than any other quarterback-receiver duo in franchise history. How many did the pair combine for?

Answers to the trivia questions are on pages 162–163

372—Favre's completions in 2005, the most ever by a Packers quarterback in a single season.

11—Quarterbacks who backed up Favre before going on to start for other teams. The list, and teams they started for, includes Don Majkowski (Indianapolis, Detroit), Ty Detmer (Philadelphia, San Francisco, Cleveland, Detroit), Mark Brunell (Jacksonville, Washington), Kurt Warner (St. Louis, New York Giants, Arizona), Doug Pederson (Philadelphia, Cleveland), Steve Bono (St. Louis), Rick Mirer (New York Jets, Oakland), Aaron Brooks (New Orleans), Matt Hasselbeck (Seattle), Danny Wuerffel (Washington), and Henry Burris (Chicago).

By the NUMBERS

-13°—The temperature at kickoff during the Ice Bowl. It was 46° below zero with the windchill. One fan died due to exposure, and several fans passed out after they warmed up. Their thawed systems had finally registered the alcohol they consumed during the game to stay warm.

Sharpe Holds
Packers Hostage

Bob Harlan remembers the roller-coaster day as though it were yesterday. It was the Saturday before the 1994 season opener, and hopes around Green Bay were sky-high. Just 24 hours before kickoff, though, star wideout Sterling Sharpe tried holding the organization hostage, saying he wouldn't play against archrival Minnesota unless the Packers renegotiated his contract.

Without a doubt, Sharpe's antics cast a black cloud over his standout Packers career, which saw him finish as Green Bay's all-time leading receiver with 595 receptions.

"In all my years, I've never been through anything like that," said Harlan, who's been Green Bay's team president since 1989. "What I remember most vividly is meeting in the draft room with [general manager] Ron Wolf and [coach] Mike Holmgren. It was a shock to all of us. It was unbelievable. But Mike talked about how we'd go and play without him and not miss a beat. It was a real positive attitude."

That attitude was formed despite fantastically difficult circumstances.

Green Bay was in the third year of the Wolf-Holmgren regime and was considered a team on the rise. But the Packers had lost four straight games to Minnesota, which was still considered the team to beat in the NFC Central.

Then, on the eve of the biggest Packers game in more than a decade, Sharpe bailed. This didn't come as a great surprise to anyone, as Sharpe had threatened such a move throughout training camp.

Sharpe said the previous administration—which included general manager Tom Braatz and head coach Lindy Infante—had given him a verbal promise to renegotiate his deal. When the new regime was slow getting to it, Sharpe took matters into his own hands.

"I think what a lot of people don't realize is Sterling had told them prior to camp that this was going to happen," former Packers linebacker Brian Noble said. "And that's really all a player has. Otherwise the team has all the power."

At 10:00 A.M. that Saturday, the Packers issued a statement saying Sharpe was displeased with his con-

tract and had left the team. Instead of having a player who caught 220 balls over the previous two seasons, Green Bay looked like it would be forced to start Ron Lewis alongside Robert Brooks against the Vikings.

"Obviously, the whole thing is a shame," a somber Holmgren said after the Packers' walk-through that day.

In 1994, the four top-paid wide receivers were San Francisco's Jerry Rice ($3 million), Tim Brown of the Los Angeles Raiders ($2.75 million), Denver's Anthony Miller ($2.6 million), and New Orleans' Michael Haynes ($2.5 million).

Sharpe was under contract through the 2000 season in a deal that averaged $1.55 million. But there was an escalator clause in the contract that bumped his salary to the average of the four highest-paid wideouts ($2.7 million) if he was selected to the Pro Bowl, named first-team All-Pro, or finished among the top three in the NFL in yards or catches.

In 1993 Sharpe hit all of the criteria, and the escalator clause kicked in. Yet he still wasn't happy with the deal he had restructured just two years earlier.

"This isn't a distraction, believe me," defensive end Sean Jones, who came from Houston that off-season, told the *Milwaukee Journal* at the time. "I came from a team where a guy shot himself to death and the defensive coordinator punched the offensive coordinator in the face.

"You guys don't know what a distraction is. They're spoiled up here. That was just business."

By the NUMBERS **20**—Ahman Green set the Packers' single-season record when he scored 20 touchdowns in 2003. Jim Taylor had 19 in 1962, and Sterling Sharpe had 18 in 1994.

GOOD THING . . . Pittsburgh's Yancey Thigpen dropped a wide-open touchdown pass in the closing seconds of a Christmas Eve game in 1995. Thigpen's drop allowed Green Bay to escape with a 24–19 win and its first NFC Central championship since 1972.

But it was much more than that to those inside the Packers family. It was a situation in which Sharpe was abandoning his teammates before a big game.

It led to a whirlwind day in which Wolf and Sharpe's agent, William "Tank" Black, talked about a new contract, and a day in which the Packers tried going on as though it were business as usual.

"Every one of our receivers is faster than Sterling," Packers quarterback Brett Favre said that day. "Now, it's just a matter if they catch the ball and make a play after it. I can't fold the tent. I'm excited."

To be honest, though, the Packers' excitement level went up a notch at about 8:00 P.M. when the team and Sharpe reached an agreement on some adjustments in his contract. The next day Sharpe lined up and caught seven passes for 53 yards and a touchdown, and Green Bay defeated the hated Vikings, 16–10.

"Please, I'm not going to say a word," Sharpe, who didn't talk to the state media, said after the game. "Nothing has changed. Talk to Mike [Holmgren]."

Sharpe would go on to have another big year, catching 94 passes and 18 touchdowns. But late that season Sharpe suffered a career-ending spinal injury.

Prior to that, however, Sharpe had lost a great deal of support in the locker room for his actions prior to the Minnesota game. Up until that point, Sharpe had been seen by most as the Packers' leader. After the fiasco, the majority of the team gravitated toward Favre. And most will tell you it has been his football team ever since.

By the NUMBERS **8,207**—Jim Taylor, who played from 1958 to 1966, has rushed for more yards than anyone else in franchise history. Ahman Green is second (7,103), and John Brockington is third (5,024).

Sterling Sharpe, who would finish his career as the Packers' all-time leading receiver, disrupted the team's chemistry with his brief holdout in 1994.

"Up until that point in time, Sterling was The Man," Noble said. "You'd get him the ball as many times as possible, and there'd be no argument with that. But people began to think the Packers were only going to go as far as Brett would take us."

In Favre's autobiography, *For the Record*, he says the change in hierarchy might have come even before Sharpe's one-day hiatus:

> The 1994 season was the year in my opinion that I became the leader on offense. Until then, Sterling was the guy. The first time I challenged him was in training camp. I had signed a four-year, $19 million contract extension in the off-season and Sterling was envious.
>
> One day in practice, I threw two bad passes in a row to him. One was high, the other was low. He came back to the huddle and said, "For $19 million, you ought to be able to put it right in my hands." I was so [upset] I started shaking.
>
> I told him, "Shut the [expletive] up and catch the ball." Everything got real quiet. I thought we were going to fight right there. Well, Sterling didn't say another word.

Instead, Sharpe let his actions do the talking a short time later when he caused one of the most tumultuous days in team history. And it's something anyone who was part of it hopes never happens again.

"It was just a shock to the entire administration," Harlan recalled. "He was one of the elite receivers in football, and we would have been in big trouble without him.

"But I couldn't have been around two better guys [Wolf and Holmgren] in that situation. The way they handled it was perfect."

A Monday Night Miracle

Al Michaels is seen as one of broadcasting's all-time greats. He did play-by-play on *Monday Night Football* for years, has called countless big games, and will long be remembered for his "Do you believe in miracles?" description of the gold medal–winning U.S. hockey team during the 1980 Olympics.

Wayne Larrivee is also regarded as one of the better broadcasters in the business. He's the radio voice of the Green Bay Packers. He calls games for the Chicago Bulls and does Big Ten football and basketball, as well.

So when both men miss a call, you know something bizarre has happened. On November 6, 2000, that something strange was Green Bay's version of the Immaculate Reception.

Green Bay defeated Minnesota that Monday night, 26–20, in overtime on a miraculous 43-yard touchdown catch by Antonio Freeman. For a few moments, though, the Lambeau Field crowd, a national television audience, and the broadcasters themselves all believed they had witnessed nothing more than an incomplete pass.

It's easy to see why looks were deceiving in this case.

Green Bay, a three-and-a-half-point underdog, got the ball first in the overtime and drove to the Minnesota 43, where it faced a third-and-four. Minnesota blitzed six, forcing Packers quarterback Brett Favre to throw off his back foot and get rid of the ball in just 1.59 seconds.

Favre took a shot deep down the right sideline for Freeman, who was working one-on-one against Minnesota cornerback Cris Dishman. Freeman slipped and fell to the ground on a field that had been getting pelted with rain, giving Dishman a clear shot at an interception.

Dishman had inside position on Freeman, and the ball hit Dishman's right hand first. It then caromed off his left hand and appeared to fall incomplete.

TOP TEN

Most Yards Passing in a Game

1.	418	Lynn Dickey vs. Tampa Bay, October 12, 1980
2.	410	Don Horn vs. St. Louis, December 21, 1969
3.	402	Brett Favre vs. Chicago, December 5, 1993
4.	399	Brett Favre vs. Oakland, December 22, 2003
5.	395	Brett Favre vs. San Francisco, October 14, 1996
6.	390	Brett Favre vs. Tampa Bay, October 10, 1999
7.	388	Brett Favre vs. Carolina, September 27, 1998
8.	387	Lynn Dickey vs. Washington, October 17, 1983
9.	384	Lynn Dickey vs. San Diego, October 7, 1984
10.	383 t	Lynn Dickey vs. Minnesota, October 23, 1983
	383 t	Brett Favre vs. Houston, November 21, 2004

"Favre puts it up for Freeman and it's incomplete," Michaels said.

Larrivee had a similar description, saying, "Favre pop fly to the right side; Freeman trying to adjust to it and it's incomplete."

Not so fast, gentlemen.

When Dishman hit the ball the second time, it ricocheted toward Freeman, who was lying facedown on the ground. The ball hit Freeman's left shoulder, and as he spun back around, the ball bounced up and he somehow managed to get his right hand underneath it.

Dishman was certain the pass was incomplete, and he jumped around, five yards behind Freeman, stewing over his failed interception. Freeman knew the ball was still alive, though, and leapt to his feet after he had secured it.

"Wait a minute," Larrivee said. "Freeman picked it up. It bounced into his hands."

It sure did. Freeman eluded safety Robert Griffith at the 14-yard line, then scurried to the end zone for one of the most improbable touchdowns you'll ever see.

The play was reviewed and upheld, marking the only time all night Green Bay had the lead. Afterward Freeman received the hero's treatment, getting carried off the field by his teammates.

"As I rolled back, I got an early Christmas gift, I guess," Freeman told reporters after the game. "Hey, who said football was all skill? Tonight, we got our lucky bounce."

It was a bounce that helped the Packers turn around their season.

Green Bay was struggling under first-year coach Mike Sherman, taking a 3–5 record into the game. Freeman's catch helped the Packers win six of their next eight games and finish 9–7.

"I wouldn't call it a miracle," Sherman said afterward. "I'd call it a happy moment. It was an even game, and we made a play at the end. It's a great win."

One that was particularly satisfying for Freeman.

Freeman had been fined $9,000 two weeks earlier for returning to Green Bay late following the Packers' bye week. He also had been going through a frustrating year on the field, seeing the ball less and less. On this night, though, Freeman not only finished with five catches for 118 yards and the game-winning touchdown, but he also came up with one of the most memorable catches in team history. In fact, a giant picture of the play hangs in the hallway leading to the Packers locker room.

"A lot of guys would have given up on that play, but Antonio stayed right with it," Sherman said. "That's the type of effort we have come to expect from him.

"I wouldn't call this redemption for Antonio Freeman. What I would call this is just a good Antonio Freeman game."

Added Freeman, "All season long, the breaks have been going against us. But tonight, we got the breaks. I just knew we weren't going to go off this field a 3–6 team."

Thanks to Freeman, they didn't.

By the NUMBERS **1,883**—In 2003 Ahman Green ran for more yards in a single season than anyone else in team history. Green broke Jim Taylor's mark of 1,474 set in 1962.

A Belated Christmas Gift

Tennessee has its Music City Miracle. Pittsburgh has the Immaculate Reception.

In Green Bay, the 2003 season will always be remembered for its belated Christmas. And playing Santa Claus for Packers fans was little-known Arizona Cardinals receiver Nathan Poole.

The Packers won their final four games of the regular season that year and finished 10–6. But hated rival Minnesota appeared well on its way to matching that record, which would have given the Vikings the NFC North division title.

Shockingly, though, Poole changed history.

In the final regular-season game, Minnesota led Arizona 17–12, and the Cardinals had a chance for one final play. There, Cardinals quarterback Josh McCown found Poole open in the back corner of the end zone and hit him for a 28-yard touchdown as time expired.

Instead of going to the playoffs, the Vikings went home. And just that fast, the Packers went from being on the outside of the postseason party to being divisional champs.

"This is like Christmas, New Year's, everything combined into one baby," safety Marques Anderson proclaimed afterward in a joyous Green Bay locker room.

"It must be Christmas on December 28," added linebacker Hannibal Navies. "Someone's looking down on us, man."

The ending capped one of the most dramatic weekends in team history, one in which Green Bay's playoff fate was in the hands of several other teams. Here's a look back on the whirlwind weekend that was for the Packers, their coaches, and their fans.

Saturday, December 27, 2003

4:15 P.M. Linebacker Na'il Diggs plops down on his couch hoping to see San Francisco upend Seattle. A Seahawks loss meant Green Bay could lose its game Sunday to Denver and still qualify for the postseason as a wild-card team.

"I was clicking in and out," Diggs said. "I was hoping the 49ers would do us a favor."

7:36 P.M. No favors for the Packers. When 49ers quarterback Jeff Garcia short-hopped a fourth-down throw, San Francisco's last chance ended. The Seahawks emerged with a 24–17 win that severely damaged Green Bay's postseason hopes.

"All the playoff scenarios and everything, I really didn't pay too much attention to those," right tackle Mark Tauscher said. "I just knew coming in [to Sunday] we needed to win."

Sunday, December 28, 2004

3:01 P.M. One thousand miles away from Lambeau Field, Minnesota and Arizona, a team with just three wins, kick off a game many consider to be just a formality. Packers fans inside Lambeau must find alternative ways to keep tabs on the game, though, as Green Bay coach Mike Sherman doesn't allow the score to be posted on any of the scoreboards inside the stadium.

3:04 P.M. The final seconds of Dallas' 13–7 loss at New Orleans tick away, meaning Green Bay's playoff hopes take another hit. Even if the Packers defeat Denver in a game about to begin, it will lose a three-way tiebreaker to Dallas and Seattle. That means the only way the Packers can reach the playoffs now is to win and have the Vikings lose.

"We knew Dallas had lost," Tauscher said. "I didn't know what the score was. I just knew they had lost."

3:15 P.M. Green Bay and Denver kick off a game that many now believe will be the Packers' final contest of the season.

4:21 P.M. Minnesota and Arizona go to halftime with the Cardinals stunning the seven-and-a-half-point favorite Vikings, 6–0.

TRIVIA

How many Packers have had their numbers retired?

Answers to the trivia questions are on pages 162–163

TOP NINE — Most 300-Yard Passing Games in a Career

1.	45	Brett Favre	1992–present
2.	15	Lynn Dickey	1976–1977, 1979–1985
3.	9	Don Majkowski	1987–1992
4.	5	Bart Starr	1956–1971
5.	2†	Tobin Rote	1950–1956
	2†	Randy Wright	1984–1988
7.	1†	Cecil Isbell	1938–1942
	1†	Don Horn	1967–1970
	1†	Mike Tomczak	1991

4:38 P.M. Green Bay is doing all it can, leading Denver 10–0 as the teams head to halftime.

4:56 P.M. Minnesota's Moe Williams plows in from one yard out, giving the Vikings their first lead of the game, 7–6.

5:26 P.M. Minnesota's lead grows to 14–6 when Dante Culpepper and Randy Moss hook up for a seven-yard touchdown with just nine minutes left in the game. That lead would grow to 17–6 at 5:34 P.M. after a 46-yard Aaron Elling field goal.

5:37 P.M. Ahman Green erupts for a 98-yard touchdown run that gives Green Bay a 24–3 lead. When James Whitley strips Adrian Madise on the ensuing kickoff and Marcus Wilkins recovers for a touchdown and a 31–3 Packers advantage, Green Bay's win is secure. All eyes turn to Minnesota.

5:53 P.M. On a fourth-and-goal play with just two minutes remaining, Cardinals quarterback Josh McCown hits tight end Steve Bush for a two-yard touchdown. The play is reviewed but stands, and Arizona closes to 17–12.

5:59 P.M. Many Packers fans inside Lambeau have switched their radios to the Vikings game, which is being carried locally. Others are trying to watch on televisions inside. They seem to be doing a pretty good job of following the action, too, because they erupt after the Cardinals' Damien Anderson recovers the onside kick.

"We didn't really know what was going on," Green Bay wide receiver Antonio Freeman said. "We just figured something good was happening when the crowd was cheering."

6:00 P.M. With the Packers' victory a foregone conclusion, media members pay little attention to what's happening on the field below. Instead, most find a television carrying the Minnesota-Arizona contest.

6:04 P.M. As the Green Bay game hits the two-minute warning, Arizona's McCown is sacked for the second straight time. With time ticking away, Arizona now scrambles to get off one final play from the Minnesota 28-yard line.

6:05 P.M. In a play Packers fans will be talking about forever, McCown takes the final snap with just 0:04 left on the clock, then avoids trouble by rolling to his right. McCown finds the little-used Poole in the right corner of the end zone. Poole makes a spectacular grab, gets one foot down, then is pushed out of bounds by Minnesota's Denard Walker and Brian Russell.

Green Bay radio announcers Wayne Larrivee and Larry McCarren have begun broadcasting the Vikings game as well. And although Sherman has done all he can to prevent the score from being known, the Lambeau Field crowd erupts at precisely the same time Poole makes his game-winning catch.

"We knew he took it off the board, and it was the same with that Dallas game, too," running back Tony Fisher said of Sherman. "But basically you just paid attention to the crowd. And when you saw the crowd erupting, you knew something good was happening."

6:08 P.M. Poole's touchdown has been under review for the allotted time, and after much deliberation, it's ruled he was forced out of bounds while making the catch and the play stands.

Green Bay's game is ending at virtually the same time, and the Packers know by watching their fans and via reports from upstairs that

By the NUMBERS **4,458**—Lynn Dickey holds the Packers' record for most passing yards in a season, a mark he set in 1983. Brett Favre ranks second (4,413 in 1995), and Don Majkowski is third (4,318 in 1989).

99—Don Hutson holds the Packers' all-time record
for receiving touchdowns. Sterling Sharpe is a distant
second with 65.

they've won the NFC North. Quarterback Brett Favre raises his arms into
the sky, then tears up. Sherman is doused with a bucket of water.
Lambeau Field becomes bedlam.

"I had no idea what was going on, and it was mad confusion," right
guard Marco Rivera said. "Then I saw the crowd react and I thought,
'What the hell's wrong with the crowd? The game's not going on. Is there
a fight over there?'

"Then I finally asked [director of football administration] Bruce
Warwick, and he said, 'Oh my God! Arizona just scored.' It was unbelievable. We were in the playoffs."

6:27 P.M. Green Bay's locker room is in chaos. Players are whooping
it up, exchanging hugs, and signing memorabilia for each other.

"It was mass hysteria, man," Navies said. "There were people running
around with hats and dancing. It was something you can't even describe.
It was such an exciting experience, and I've never been part of anything
like that."

Poole becomes such a hero in Green Bay that he's invited to the
Packers' wild-card game with Seattle the following weekend and given
the grand tour by Green Bay's mayor.

"Oh, we've got to get him something," wideout Donald Driver said of
Poole. "As a receiving corps, we've got to take care of him. That cat saved
our season."

And capped one of the more incredible 24-hour stretches in team
history.

Fourth-and-26

Three words. Three painful little words.

They'll be part of Packers lore long after Ed Donatell has left this world. And they'll stick with members of the 2003–2004 Green Bay Packers defense for the rest of time.

Fourth-and-26.

Those three words say it all. And the mere mention of them causes Packers fans agonizing, depressing, and torturous flashbacks.

"Let's not sugarcoat it," said Donatell, Green Bay's defensive coordinator at the time. "It's part of Packers history. They'll talk about it for a long, long time."

Boy, will they ever.

The date was January 11, 2004. Green Bay was playing Philadelphia in the NFC divisional playoffs for the right to meet Carolina in the NFC championship game. With 1:12 left in the contest, the Packers led 17–14, and Philadelphia faced a fourth-and-26 from its own 26-yard line.

Green Bay sat in a Cover 2 defense and rushed four. When the pressure was nonexistent, the middle of the field was wide open.

Nick Barnett, Green Bay's middle linebacker, had failed to get a deep enough drop with wideout Freddie Mitchell. Safeties Marques Anderson and Darren Sharper had inexplicably fallen 30 yards deep into coverage.

Philadelphia quarterback Donovan McNabb fired a dart to Mitchell, and when nickel back Bhawoh Jue made a poor play on the ball and both safeties arrived late, Mitchell picked up 28 yards and the most impossible of first downs.

Just moments later, Philadelphia won the game in overtime, 20–17. And the words *fourth-and-26* would live in infamy around Green Bay.

"That thing's never going to go away because its part of history now," said Sharper, who was the main culprit in Terrell Owens' game-winning TD catch in a 30–27 loss to San Francisco in a 1998 wild-card game. "Similar to the play in the San Francisco playoff game. Those plays are a part of history, so they're always going to be replayed. That's how you [media members] operate."

How Green Bay operated on that fateful play will still pain Packers fans years from now.

The Packers had played fantastic defense against McNabb and the Eagles all day. And they appeared in sensational shape to reach their first NFC title game since 1997.

Philadelphia wide receiver Freddie Mitchell celebrates his 28-yard reception in front of the Packers' Al Harris on January 11, 2004.

Trailing, 17–14, the Eagles had the ball at their own 42-yard line with two minutes left. On first down, Sharper blitzed from his safety position and knocked down McNabb's pass.

On second down, Jue came on a blitz and sacked McNabb for a 16-yard loss. After McNabb threw incomplete deep down the seam for tight end Chad Lewis on third down, the Eagles were left staring at a fourth-and-26 with 1:12 remaining.

TRIVIA

Through 2005, which Packers player had been named to the most Pro Bowls?

Answers to the trivia questions are on pages 162–163

Green Bay seemed disorganized, much like it had been the previous week during overtime of its wild-card game against Seattle. There, the Packers called timeout, and on the ensuing play, Al Harris intercepted a Matt Hasselbeck pass and returned it for the game-winning touchdown.

This time, though, the Packers bypassed the timeout, something several questioned afterward.

"Quite frankly, we should have called a timeout," cornerback Michael Hawthorne said. "We should have called timeout to regroup and play the defense that we know will make them catch everything in front of us. We had the timeout, but it was a brain freeze on the sideline. If I didn't know what to do there, I would have called a timeout. That was crucial. That could have catapulted us to the next step."

Instead, the Packers' season was over only minutes later.

A math professor at the University of Wisconsin–Green Bay later calculated the odds of the Eagles converting the play based on several factors. Under one formula, Philadelphia's chances were 1-in-339 of picking up the first down.

Those proved to be rough odds for Donatell. Just five days after the play took place, Packers coach Mike Sherman fired Donatell, in essence making him the scapegoat. To this day, Donatell insists he wouldn't have done anything differently. He would just have coached it better.

"I'd coach Nick Barnett to stay back deeper, I'd tell Bhawoh Jue to have awareness, and I'd tell Darren Sharper to buy that route at 20 yards," Donatell said. "But I'm not blaming any player. I'm not blaming any assistant. The buck stops with me. Somewhere along the line, the buck's got to stop, and it's stopping right on me. I'm blaming myself for the way that was coached."

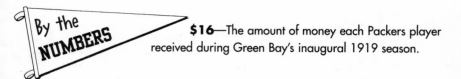

$16—The amount of money each Packers player received during Green Bay's inaugural 1919 season.

Donatell landed on his feet, accepting the defensive coordinator's job in Atlanta less than 48 hours after Sherman whacked him. The following season, Donatell and the Falcons reached the NFC championship game.

"When something like that happens and you're only singled out because you're the only guy asked to leave, you could say it's an indictment on your coaching," Donatell said. "Then you've got to prove 'em wrong. I've taken just one step to doing that in what we're doing in Atlanta. I think there will be more good things to follow.

"I know there was a ton of support when it happened, and right now there's a lot of guys that are happy for our success in Atlanta. You wouldn't believe the outreach of support. Guys come up to me, guys I don't even know, and say nice things."

Meanwhile, Green Bay's defense took a major step backward the following season, and Sherman fired defensive coordinator Bob Slowik—Donatell's replacement—at the end of the 2004 campaign.

Several of the players involved in fourth-and-26 were also jettisoned shortly thereafter. Anderson didn't return the next season, while Sharper, Hawthorne, and Jue each left after the 2004 campaign.

And it's safe to say, the stigma of that play will follow them wherever they go.

"Man, even in the Bahamas I was hearing about it," Harris said. "Everywhere I went it was all fourth-and-26. And there's nothing you can do. It was the play that was called."

"I wasn't even on the field, but people still bring it up," former Packers guard Mike Wahle said. "What are you going to do. [Expletive] happens. It was a bad play."

One of the worst in franchise history. And one that will be talked about for generations to come.

A President Few Would Impeach

The love of Bob Harlan's life has always been his wife, Madeline. Heck, they've been married for nearly 50 years and have three sons and four grandchildren.

But if it's possible for a grown man to have nearly as much affection for an NFL franchise, Harlan is living proof.

During Harlan's days as a student at Marquette University in the fifties, he would hitchhike down Wisconsin Avenue to watch the Green Bay Packers play at County Stadium. He traveled to Wrigley Field to see Green Bay play the hated Chicago Bears. And, of course, he's been the Packers president since 1989, overseeing a return to glory on the field and spearheading the renovation of Lambeau Field, which helped rescue the team financially.

For his efforts, Harlan was inducted into the Packers Hall of Fame in 2004. And the argument can certainly be made that he's the finest president in Packers history.

"He was great to work for," Ron Wolf, Green Bay's general manager from 1991 to 2000, said of Harlan. "He did exactly what he promised. He put me in charge of the football operations and never once did he interfere. I think he did a lot for the Packers' operations, and the Packers are back on the map because of it."

One could argue that Harlan has been as influential as any president in team history. Harlan joined the organization in 1971 as an assistant general manager and rose through the ranks, eventually becoming the Packers' ninth president in 1989. Since that time, Harlan has been the driving force behind some of the largest moves in franchise history.

His greatest success on the field was the hiring of Wolf as the team's GM in 1991. Wolf proceeded to hire Mike Holmgren as coach

TOP TEN

Most Receptions in a Season

1.	112	Sterling Sharpe	1993
2.	108	Sterling Sharpe	1992
3.	102	Robert Brooks	1995
4.	94	Sterling Sharpe	1994
5.	90	Sterling Sharpe	1989
6.	89	Javon Walker	2004
7.	86	Donald Driver	2005
8.	84 †	Donald Driver	2004
	84 †	Antonio Freeman	1998
10.	81	Antonio Freeman	1997

and surround him with a talent-laden roster led by Brett Favre and Reggie White.

Those moves helped the Packers win Super Bowl XXXI and NFC championships in 1996 and 1997. In fact, Green Bay went from 1992 to 2004 without a losing season, an amazing accomplishment in the era of free agency and the salary cap.

Off the field, the time Harlan spent campaigning for the stadium referendum in 2000 matched what any politician goes through. For eight months Harlan spent the majority of his waking hours making appearances, shaking hands, and lobbying for the renovation of Lambeau Field.

The measure eventually passed by a 53–47 margin, drawing $169.1 million in public funds to complement the $135.9 million the Packers ponied up. The $295 million project increased the stadium's capacity from 60,890 to 72,601 and has helped the Packers move from the bottom third of the league in revenue to the top third.

Ask Harlan what he's most proud of, though, and it's like choosing between filet mignon and Boston lobster.

"If I said the biggest thing football-wise, obviously it's winning the Super Bowl because we restored credibility to this corporation in a hurry," said Harlan, who worked in public relations at Marquette University and with the St. Louis Cardinals before coming to the Packers. "And the biggest thing off the field had to be the stadium because we had to have it. It was a battle to get it done. But once we did it—and this is what gives me a great deal of pleasure—the stadium is doing exactly what we told the voters that it would do.

"It elevated this franchise in revenue, it's going to keep us a viable part of the NFL, and it's bringing visitors to Green Bay and Brown County from around the world, literally. It's bringing a lot of people in, and I guess that's what really pleases me. We told the voters this is what it would do and it's doing it."

While those are the crowning jewels of Harlan's career, he's had several other landmark moves.

Harlan helped launch the fourth stock sale in team history in 1997, a move that produced more than $20 million of "new money" and more than one hundred thousand new shareholders. He authorized the construction of the Don Hutson Center, giving Green Bay one of the league's top indoor practice facilities. He presided over the Packers' controversial decision to stop playing home games in Milwaukee in 1994. And in January 2005, he stripped Packers coach Mike Sherman of his general manager duties and hired Ted Thompson to fill that role.

Through it all, Harlan has remained the rarest of executives and still picks up his own phone when "Joe Six Pack" calls.

"I like to avoid all the confusion of going through secretaries if people are trying to reach me," Harlan said. "And secondly, I feel like I owe the fans that. I think since these people own this team, if they want to reach me, they should be able to do so. I don't want them saying, 'Well, you can't find Harlan.' Well, yes you can. I answered the phone those eight months we were going through the referendum. I wasn't always happy to answer the phone, but I did it.

"And I get letters from fans now, and if they have a legitimate complaint or problem, I'll call them when they come home from work that night. And first of all, they're surprised I took the time to read their letter. Then they're really surprised I took the time to call because they didn't give me their phone number. Some of them say, 'How did you reach me?' And I say, 'Well, I called information.' But I like to talk to the fans. We just

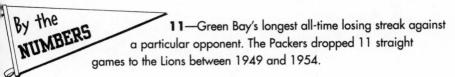

By the NUMBERS 11—Green Bay's longest all-time losing streak against a particular opponent. The Packers dropped 11 straight games to the Lions between 1949 and 1954.

TRIVIA

What was Tony Canadeo's nickname?

A. Grey Ghost
B. Night Train
C. White Shadow
D. Flash

Answers to the trivia questions are on pages 162–163

don't ignore things. I just don't want people feeling we're sitting up on this high hill, sold out, and don't have time for anybody."

Harlan has certainly made his time in Green Bay memorable, which is why it will be tough for him to say good-bye. Harlan will turn 70 on September 9, 2006, an age at which team bylaws say a president must retire.

Although that day won't be easy, Harlan is grateful for the time he has had running one of America's most storied organizations.

"This was a longtime fan situation for me, even before I got here," Harlan said. "When I was in St. Louis for baseball, I was very happy there and loved the Cardinal organization. But the chance to come to Green Bay was very, very attractive for my wife and myself.

"It turned out to be a great place to raise our children, and it's a great family atmosphere. I've always said that this is the best story going in sports because of the uniqueness. And even fighting for the stadium, I found out I love the stadium as much as I love the team. It's been a wonderful thing for me."

It's been even better for the Packers.

By the NUMBERS 9,901—James Lofton holds the team record for most yards from scrimmage in a career. Jim Taylor is second (9,712), and Ahman Green is third (9,438).

The Minister of Defense Rests

The man seemed downright invincible at times. He had one of the most unique size-to-speed ratios the National Football League had ever seen. He treated offensive linemen like rag dolls for 60 minutes each Sunday, then like family afterward. He was one of the greatest leaders the sports world has ever known, a man whose raspy voice was legendary and whose words were even more important. He conquered injuries that would have sidelined most mortals and led his beloved Green Bay Packers to the pinnacle. And through it all, he stayed true to faith, family, and football.

Yes, at times Reggie White was larger than life, which is why the news of his death on December 26, 2004, at just 43 years old, shocked not only those around the NFL, but everyone White ever came in contact with.

"It just seems so odd, so surreal," former teammate Eugene Robinson told the *Milwaukee Journal Sentinel*. "I'm still like, 'I don't believe it.' When I saw it flash on the television—1961 to 2004—I was just like, 'I'm not going to try to fight back any more tears. I'm just going to cry.'"

According to the medical examiner's office in Mecklenburg County, North Carolina, White died of an irregular heartbeat that was caused by an inflammatory condition called sarcoidosis in his lungs and heart. The medical examiner also said White suffered from sleep apnea, which could have been a contributing factor.

"I was shocked," Green Bay quarterback Brett Favre said. "He was a great friend of mine and a great friend of my family's.

"It's hard to think that he is gone. I had the utmost respect for Reggie White as a player. He may have been the best player I've ever seen and certainly was the best I've ever played with or against."

Packers fans wouldn't argue.

When the discussion of Green Bay's turnaround in the nineties comes up, five men are typically given the lion's share of the credit: team president Bob Harlan, general manager Ron Wolf, coach Mike Holmgren, Favre, and White.

While viewpoints differ as to which individual played the largest role in Green Bay's rise to prominence, a case can easily be made for White.

TRIVIA

Who is Green Bay's all-time leading scorer?

Answers to the trivia questions are on pages 162–163

White's signing on April 6, 1993, shocked the football world and gave Green Bay arguably the league's most dominant defensive end and an instant dose of credibility.

White made it all right to play in the NFL's smallest city, one many players dreaded coming to up until that time. But most important, White's signing helped transform Green Bay's defense from a second-tier bunch in 1993 to the number one unit in the NFL by 1996.

"That's what changed the football fortunes of this franchise," Harlan said. "It was huge. Everyone thought the last place he would sign was Green Bay, and it was monumental because not only did he sign but he recruited for Green Bay and got guys like Sean Jones to come here. He sent a message to the rest of the NFL that Green Bay was a great place to play."

Added Wolf, "You can argue all day about what the biggest move was. But in some order, it's Mike, Brett, and Reggie. Reggie helped clear the way for us to sign other free agents. With what he did on and off the field, he earned every bit of that contract."

White's deal, which pales in comparison to many today, was fantastically gaudy at the time. He signed with Green Bay for four years and $17 million that included a $4.5 million signing bonus and paid out $9 million in the first year.

White immediately became the third-highest-paid player in league history, trailing only Denver's John Elway ($4.775 million) and Miami's Dan Marino ($4.43 million).

"We've improved our defense dramatically," Wolf said at the time. "Realistically, the best step we've made was the hiring of Mike Holmgren. But this is a very key move."

The Packers weren't even on White's initial radar screen, but when he visited Detroit in early March, he stopped by Green Bay because he was in the neighborhood and the Packers had been extremely persistent. White met with Holmgren, defensive coordinator Ray Rhodes, and defensive line coach Greg Blache, but it still appeared as though the Packers stood little chance to win the White sweepstakes.

The following week, however, Holmgren and Rhodes flew to White's home in Knoxville, Tennessee, to meet with White and his family. That impressed White, but Green Bay's blockbuster contract offer did much of the talking.

Green Bay's deal exceeded offers from San Francisco, Washington, and Cleveland, and eventually, White decided to become a Packer. And when he put his name on the dotted line, it became one of the more momentous days in franchise history.

"We shocked the world, didn't we?" White's agent, Jimmy Sexton, said at the time.

"I feel the dollars offered by Green Bay were just far too much to overcome," San Francisco 49ers president Carmen Policy said at the

Reggie White contributed greatly to the organization and the community as a whole during his tenure in Green Bay.

TOP TEN

Most Receiving Yards in a Season

1.	1,497	Robert Brooks	1995
2.	1,461	Sterling Sharpe	1992
3.	1,424	Antonio Freeman	1998
4.	1,423	Sterling Sharpe	1989
5.	1,382	Javon Walker	2004
6.	1,361	James Lofton	1984
7.	1,300	James Lofton	1983
8.	1,294	James Lofton	1981
9.	1,274	Sterling Sharpe	1993
10.	1,243	Antonio Freeman	1997

time. "Without guaranteeing the contract, which we wouldn't do, we couldn't come close to matching the deal."

As teams throughout the league recruited White, he spoke of his faith and how God would guide him in the right direction. At his introductory press conference, it was no surprise White again referenced his faith.

"A lot of people really questioned me when I said I had to wait and see where God wants me to be," White said. "The situation came down to where I had to feel peace about where I wanted to be. And I had to have a sound mind about where I wanted to be. You know, the Bible says God is not of confusion, but of peace and a sound mind. That's what I was looking for, and I've gotten peace about being here and a sound mind about being here."

While White got the peace he was looking for, the Packers got an ultimate difference maker. Even at the age of 31, White could take over a game like few other players.

In the seven years before White's arrival, he had 111 sacks with Philadelphia. In that same time, Green Bay's entire defensive line had 80.5 sacks.

White was named to the Pro Bowl every year between 1986 and 1992 and was named the NFL's Defensive Player of the Year in 1991 by *Pro Football Weekly*. His 124 career sacks trailed only Lawrence Taylor (126.5).

White also proved prophetic at his introductory press conference.

"Me and Coach made an agreement. We're going to the Super Bowl, aren't we?" White said to Holmgren. "Green Bay is the team that really started off the championships. And I think if this team could get back to a winning attitude, to a championship, I think it could capture the heart of America."

And that is exactly what happened. After a pair of 9–7 seasons that ended in the divisional playoffs, Green Bay went 11–5 and reached the NFC championship game in 1995. Then in 1996, Green Bay dominated the league, outscoring its foes 456–210 and ranking first in both offense and defense on its way to a 35–21 victory over New England in Super Bowl XXXI.

One of White's finest moments in a Packers uniform came during the Super Bowl victory, when he consistently abused Patriots right tackle Max Lane. White finished the game with three sacks and helped bring Green Bay its first championship in 29 years.

"God sent me here," White said after that game. "Some of you guys thought I was crazy four years ago, but now I'm getting a ring. How crazy do you think I am now?"

White would play with the Packers through 1998, finishing with 68.5 sacks in his six years, which ranks first in team history.

As dominant as White was on the field, he was equally productive off it. White, who was named to the Pro Bowl each of his six seasons in Green Bay, would often use that time to try convincing free agents of why Green Bay would be a perfect home for them. And after the Packers traded for tight end Keith Jackson, who didn't want to play in Green Bay, White persuaded him to come. Jackson was happy he did, as he wound up being a key cog on the Super Bowl championship team.

White, an ordained minister from the time he was 17, had a few trying moments during his time in Green Bay. In 1996 a church in Knoxville, Tennessee, that White was once associated with burned.

By the NUMBERS

6'8"—Ben Davidson, Bill Hayhoe, and Vernon Vanoy are the tallest players to ever play in a game for Green Bay. Davidson was a defensive end–tackle in 1961, Hayhoe was an offensive tackle from 1969 to 1973, and Vanoy was a defensive tackle in 1972.

TRIVIA

How many fields has Green Bay called home in addition to Lambeau Field?

Answers to the trivia questions are on pages 162–163

Roughly $250,000 was raised—mostly by Packers fans that appreciated what White had meant to the team. But the church was never rebuilt and the money never recovered, which damaged White's reputation. Then, following a trip to Israel in 1998, White was invited to speak in front of the Wisconsin State Assembly. There, he called homosexuality a sin and made critical remarks about several different ethnic groups. That speech cost him a job as a network television analyst and probably several endorsement deals as well. But for the most part, his time in Green Bay was a rousing success.

White finished his career with 198 sacks, which ranks second all time behind Bruce Smith (200). He was a first-ballot Hall of Fame selection in 2006 and was inducted into the Packers' Hall of Fame as well.

"Playing with Reggie was one of the highlights of my career," Robinson said of White. "He was one of the big reasons I was so happy to get traded to Green Bay.

"A great man. A great football player. A great leader. Playing with him was outstanding."

General Sherman

R-i-n-ggggg. R-i-n-ggggg. R-i-n-ggggg. Packers coach Mike Sherman was in the middle of a rather nondescript midweek press conference halfway through the 2005 season. Green Bay was a miserable 1–6 at the time. Sherman's job was on the line. And his patience had almost expired.

In the back of the auditorium, where a cavalcade of cameramen was filming the event, a cell phone went off. Within nanoseconds, Sherman blew his top.

Sherman, who was in the middle of talking about his defense, stopped mid-sentence. He stormed off the stage on which he had been speaking, lectured the gathered media, then exited stage left.

Although Sherman didn't know it at the time, he could have kept walking. His own phone was about to be unplugged.

Just two months later, Green Bay general manager Ted Thompson fired Sherman.

Thompson, who had replaced Sherman as Green Bay's GM one year earlier, named little-known San Francisco offensive coordinator Mike McCarthy to be the Packers' 14th head coach.

"Decisions like this are never easy," Thompson said the day he fired Sherman. "They require a lot of thought and consternation, but at the end of the day, I thought we needed to go in a different direction."

Sherman's ouster ended a six-year run (2000–2005) that Green Bay fans will look back on as one of the most unfulfilling tenures in team history.

Sherman was a workaholic who did some good things, such as winning three straight NFC North division titles between 2002 and 2004. He also posted a .594 winning percentage (57–39) that ranks fourth all time among Packers coaches.

TOP TEN — Most Consecutive Games Played

1.	223	Brett Favre	1992–2005
2.	187	Forrest Gregg	1956, 1958–1970
3.	166	Willie Wood	1960–1971
4.	162	Larry McCarren	1973–1984
5.	150	Boyd Dowler	1959–1969
6.	144	Ryan Longwell	1997–2005
7.	140	Fred Carr	1968–1977
8.	138	Bill Forester	1953–1963
9.	136†	Willie Davis	1960–1969
	136†	James Lofton	1978–1986

But Sherman will be forever known in Green Bay as the man who couldn't get the Packers over the hump.

Sherman inherited Hall of Fame quarterback Brett Favre, who was in the absolute prime of his career. And just three months after Sherman was named head coach, then-Packers general manager Ron Wolf hoodwinked Seattle and traded for running back Ahman Green.

During the first five years of Sherman's tenure, Favre and Green were arguably football's best quarterback–running back tandem and were named to a combined seven Pro Bowls. The defense was respectable, and the team included Pro Bowl pass catchers in Javon Walker, Donald Driver, and Bubba Franks.

But under Sherman's watch Green Bay didn't even reach an NFC championship game. The Packers were a disappointing 2–4 in the postseason. They lost the first two home playoff games in franchise history—to Atlanta in 2002 and Minnesota in 2004. And they suffered their most lopsided playoff defeat ever, a 45–17 setback to St. Louis in 2001.

"We had some trouble in the playoffs," Driver said. "Some really bad losses."

Sherman's legacy came via the 2003 NFC divisional playoffs. And it wasn't one to be proud of.

The Packers led Philadelphia, 17–14, with 2:30 left and had a fourth-and-one at the Eagles' 41-yard line. At his disposal, Sherman had arguably the finest offensive line in team history and a running back in Green that had shattered virtually every single-season rushing record in Packers history that season.

Green Bay had also averaged 5.68 yards per carry throughout the game that day. And Philadelphia's defensive line was both beat up and worn out.

Instead of distributing the knockout punch, though, Sherman lost his nerve.

He elected to punt. Philadelphia converted the legendary fourth-and-26 and eventually won the game, 20–17, in overtime.

Departed head coach Mike Sherman shares a friendly moment with wide receiver Robert Ferguson during minicamp prior to the 2004 season.

TOP TEN

Most Receiving Yards in a Game

1.	257	Billy Howton vs. Los Angeles Rams October 21, 1956
2.	237	Don Hutson at Brooklyn Dodgers November 21, 1943
3.	220	Don Beebe vs. San Francisco 49ers October 14, 1996
4.	209	Don Hutson vs. Cleveland Rams October 18, 1942
5.	207 t	Don Hutson vs. Chicago Cardinals November 1, 1942
	207 t	Don Hutson vs. Card-Pitt October 8, 1944
7.	206	James Lofton at Denver Broncos October 15, 1984
8.	205	Carroll Dale vs. Detroit Lions September 29, 1968
9.	200 t	Billy Howton at Los Angeles Rams December 7, 1952
	200 t	Javon Walker at Indianapolis Colts September 26, 2004

"You don't think we could have got a [expletive] yard?" Packers guard Mike Wahle said months later. "Give me a break."

From that point on, it was all downhill for Sherman.

Sherman had been named Green Bay's general manager before the 2001 season, when Wolf abruptly retired. Packers general manager Bob Harlan didn't care for one person holding both jobs, but he went against his better judgment and added the GM role to Sherman's coaching duties.

For a few seasons, Sherman lived well off the abundance of talent Wolf had stockpiled. But eventually Sherman's miserable decisions as GM—such as signing free agent flop Joe Johnson, trading up to draft punter B. J. Sander in the third round, and missing on first-round picks such as Jamal Reynolds and Ahmad Carroll—began to leave the roster barren.

And after the Packers lost to Minnesota in the 2004 playoffs, Harlan stripped Sherman of the general manager role and hired Thompson to replace him.

"I don't want the word criticism to be a part of this," Harlan said when announcing Thompson's hiring. "I don't want us to falter. I want us to stay strong. And that's where this is coming from.

"To criticize [Sherman], I don't think is the right way to approach it. I told him, 'This is help. This is not criticism.'"

Although Harlan wouldn't criticize Sherman, others seemed to be lining up to do so.

During Sherman's time in Green Bay, he had gone from a somewhat humble man to one that was downright egomaniacal. Many on Sherman's coaching staff

New Packers head coach Mike McCarthy, a former assistant, is introduced to the media on January 12, 2006.

complained that he didn't listen to their input and simply did things his own way.

And after the 2004 season, some, such as running backs coach Johnny Roland and receivers coach Ray Sherman, accepted lateral moves with losing teams.

"The head coach thought he was the only one with any brains," said Roland, who had 26 years of NFL experience. "There was a lot of collective knowledge in the people that have left. And that knowledge wasn't listened to.

"There were a lot of guys that have been around a long time. You think they should have a little bit of input into how this game should be played and things you should take advantage of. But that wasn't how it worked up there."

Jeff Jagodzinski was Green Bay's tight ends coach under Sherman from 2000 to 2003 but was fired in large part because he was one of the few coaches to stand up to Sherman. Jagodzinski, who was quickly hired by Atlanta, agreed wholeheartedly with Roland.

"Why do you think those guys left?" said Jagodzinski, who was later hired as McCarthy's offensive coordinator. "It wasn't to go to a better team. It's because in Green Bay, your ideas don't get listened to. In Green Bay, a lot of guys bite their tongues on a lot of things.

"If you're in an organization, you want to feel that you're a part of it. And when you don't have any decision-making responsibilities or they don't take your suggestions or whatever, that's frustrating."

The frustration only grew for Sherman in 2005. The Packers had their worst season since 1991, going a disappointing 4–12.

And when Sherman arrived for work the day after the season finale, Thompson fired him. Later that week, Sherman met with the media one final time and showed a rare sense of humor.

"Hope you all put away your cell phones," he joked. "Don't need to go back there."

No one was arguing.

Brett's Back

General Hospital. Days of Our Lives. As the World Turns.

Each of these soap operas certainly contains plenty of drama for its respective fan base. But in recent years, the Green Bay Packers have been forced to live with their own soap opera.

The title? *As Brett Favre Waffles.*

Favre, Green Bay's soon-to-be Hall of Fame quarterback, began hinting at retirement all the way back in the 2002 season. Each off-season, Favre has taken longer than the one before it to decide whether or not he'll play another year.

In 2006, though, Favre set a personal record for indecisiveness.

From the time the 2005 regular season ended to the time Favre made up his mind, a remarkable 113 days passed. Finally, Favre phoned Packers general manager Ted Thompson and informed him he'd return for a 15th season in Green Bay.

"I would have rather had it a couple of months ago," Thompson said of Favre's decision. "But that's OK."

Favre is without question the most popular Packer of this era and one of the most beloved players in team history. But his annual uncertainty has rubbed many the wrong way and has become a tired story each off-season.

Favre took his sweet time following the 2005 season to see what moves Thompson would make to improve a Packers team that had just concluded a 4–12 season—the first losing team Favre had been a part of in Green Bay. But the longer Favre waited, the more disappointed he became.

Thompson, who believes in building a team through the draft, elected to do little in free agency simply to appease Favre. And the

TOP TEN

Most Touchdown Receptions in a Season

1.	18	Sterling Sharpe	1994
2.	17	Don Hutson	1942
3.	14	Antonio Freeman	1998
4.	13*t*	Billy Howton	1952
	13*t*	Sterling Sharpe	1992
	13*t*	Robert Brooks	1995
7.	12*t*	Billy Howton	1956
	12*t*	Sterling Sharpe	1989
	12*t*	Antonio Freeman	1997
	12*t*	Javon Walker	2004

legendary quarterback, who spends his off-seasons at his Hattiesburg, Mississippi, home, watched from afar while going back and forth on his future.

"I guess ultimately it comes down to just whether or not you want to play and run the risk of being 4–12," Favre said. "There's always that risk, just as there is a chance of us being 12–4. I never thought we would ever go 4–12 in my tenure here in Green Bay, and we did. Nothing surprises me anymore. That's something I have to live with, if I'm willing to go through that again."

Eventually Favre decided he was willing to go through that again. And it could make for a record-breaking 2006 season.

Favre, who already holds the NFL record for most consecutive starts by a quarterback (221), is closing in on several other hallowed marks as well. With 396 career touchdown passes, he's just 24 shy of Dan Marino's all-time record. Favre's 4,678 career completions are second to Marino (4,967). And with 139 career wins, he's third behind John Elway (148) and Marino (147).

By the NUMBERS

15—Green Bay's longest all-time winning streak against a particular opponent. The Packers defeated the Chicago Cardinals 15 straight times between 1937 and 1946. Green Bay's second-best streak was 10 straight wins over the Chicago Bears between 1994 and 1998.

With a big year in 2006, Favre could capture every one of those records.

"He could accomplish some really big things," wide receiver Donald Driver said. "I mean he can break records that most people thought would never be broken."

TRIVIA

Who has the most touchdowns in Packers history?

Answers to the trivia questions are on pages 162–163

Anyone that knows Favre, though, realizes records aren't what drive him. Instead, it's that quest for another Super Bowl title. With the Packers in a rebuilding mode, the odds of achieving that goal are infinitesimal. But Green Bay's chances of winning are certainly better with Favre than without him.

"Having Brett Favre is absolutely a good thing," Thompson said. "And we're very happy he is [back]."

So is Packer Nation. They just wish he'd start figuring it out a little faster.

Green Bay's Fantastic 50

Packers historian Lee Remmel ranks the top 50 players in team history. Here's a look at that list and a glimpse at each individual's career.

1. Don Hutson, E/DB, 1935–1945: Set 18 records during his brilliant playing days, including 10 that still stand. Hutson, who had breakaway speed, was credited with inventing pass patterns and led the league in receiving eight times and scoring five times. He was inducted into the Pro Football Hall of Fame in 1963.
2. Bart Starr, QB, 1956–1971: Never flashy, just successful. Starr led Green Bay to five world championships, including two Super Bowls, along with six western division titles. He was named to four Pro Bowls and led the league in passing three times. He later coached the Packers from 1975 to 1983 and was named to the Hall of Fame in 1977.
3. Brett Favre, QB, 1992–present: Ranks second in NFL history in touchdown passes (396) and completions (4,678) and third in passing yards (53,615). Favre's 221 consecutive starts are an all-time record for quarterbacks and a Packers team mark. Favre is the league's only three-time Most Valuable Player, and he guided the Packers to the 1996 Super Bowl championship.
4. Paul Hornung, RB/K, 1957–1962, 1964–1966: Won the NFL scoring title from 1959 to 1961 and established an all-time league scoring mark with 176 points in 1960. A two-time Pro Bowl pick and twice an All-Pro, Hornung was suspended during the 1963 season for gambling. He was elected to the Hall of Fame in 1986.
5. Forrest Gregg, T, 1956, 1958–1970: A nine-time Pro Bowl player and an eight-time All-Pro selection. Gregg was called the "finest player I

ever coached" by Lombardi. He is second in team history with 187 consecutive starts and was the Packers' head coach from 1984 to 1987. Gregg was named to the Hall of Fame in 1977.

6. Ray Nitschke, LB, 1958–1972: Ferocious player named to the NFL's All–50 Year Team and the 75th Anniversary Team, Nitschke was the MVP of Green Bay's win in the 1962 title game and was elected to the Hall of Fame in 1978.

7. Clarke Hinkle, FB, 1932–1941: A punishing runner who ranks sixth in Packers history with 3,860 yards. Hinkle was named to the NFL All-Pro team four times and was selected to the NFL's All-Time Two-Way Team in 1994. He was named to the Hall of Fame in 1964.

8. Willie Wood, FS, 1960–1971: One of just six nondrafted free agents to reach the Hall of Fame (1989). Wood was named to eight Pro Bowls and helped the Packers win five NFL titles. His interception and 50-yard return to Kansas City's 5-yard line helped break open a close game in Super Bowl I. He led the NFL with nine picks in 1962 and was a splendid punt returner who won the crown in 1961 with a 16.1 average.

9. Robert "Cal" Hubbard, T, 1929–1933, 1935: At 6'5", 250 pounds, was massive for his era. Also a standout defensive player, Hubbard was selected to the NFL's All–50 Year Team in 1970 and its All-Time Two-Way Team in 1994. He was elected to the Hall of Fame in 1963.

Ray Nitschke was one of the league's toughest, meanest, and most feared defenders ever.

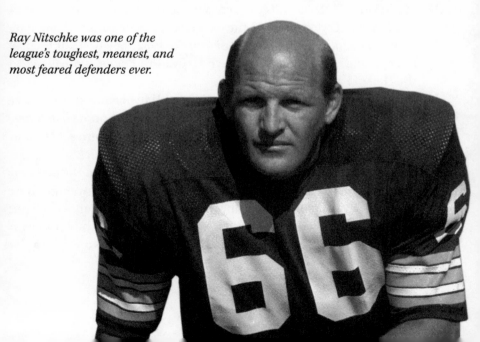

10. Tony Canadeo, HB, 1941–1944, 1946–1952: Nicknamed the "Grey Ghost," Canadeo ranks fourth in team history in rushing yards (4,197). He was just the NFL's third 1,000-yard rusher when he went for 1,052 yards in 1949. Named to the Hall of Fame in 1974, Canadeo served Green Bay's organization for 59 years, longer than anyone in team history, before his death in 2003.

11. Herb Adderley, DB, 1961–1969: Five-time All-Pro cornerback and five-time Pro Bowl selection. Adderley, who also played for Dallas, had 39 of his 48 career interceptions as a Packer and ran seven back for touchdowns. He was named to the Hall of Fame in 1980.

12. Reggie White, DE, 1993–1998: Biggest free-agent signing in Green Bay's history. White didn't disappoint. He set the franchise record with 68.5 sacks in his six years with the Packers and ranks second in NFL history in career sacks. He had three sacks in Super Bowl XXXI, helping the Packers beat New England, 35–21. He was named to the Pro Football Hall of Fame in 2006.

13. Henry Jordan, DT, 1959–1969: Came to the Packers in a trade with Cleveland in 1959. Jordan was named All-Pro from 1960 to 1964 and was a four-time Pro Bowl selection. He had 3.5 sacks in Green Bay's 1967 Western Conference championship win over the Los Angeles Rams and was named to the Hall of Fame in 1995.

14. Jim Taylor, FB, 1958–1966: Green Bay's all-time leading rusher with 8,207 yards. Taylor eclipsed the 1,000-yard rushing mark from 1960 to 1964, including a 1,474-yard season in 1962 that was a franchise record for 41 years. He was named to five Pro Bowls and elected to the Hall of Fame in 1976.

15. Willie Davis, DE, 1960–1969: Named to the Hall of Fame in 1981 after being named to five Pro Bowls and earning All-Pro honors five times. He is Green Bay's all-time leader in fumble recoveries (21) and helped the Packers win five championships in the sixties.

16. Jerry Kramer, G, 1958–1968: Combined with center Ken Bowman on the most famous block in NFL history, clearing the way for Bart Starr's one-yard touchdown run with 16 seconds left that gave Green Bay a 21–17 win in the 1967 NFL championship game, better known as the Ice Bowl. Kramer was named to three Pro Bowls and was a six-time All-Pro.

17. Jim Ringo, C, 1953–1963: Eight-time All-Pro and 10-time Pro Bowl player, seven as a Packer. Ringo helped Green Bay win back-to-back titles in 1961 and 1962 and once held the NFL record for consecutive games played (183). He was traded to Philadelphia in 1964 and named to the Hall of Fame in 1981.

18. James Lofton, WR, 1978–1986: Green Bay's first-round draft choice in 1978. Lofton's 9,656 receiving yards as a Packer rank first in team history, and his 530 receptions are second. He also played for the Los Angeles Raiders, Buffalo, Los Angeles Rams, and Philadephia and was an eight-time Pro Bowl selection. In 2003 Lofton became the first Packer Hall of Famer since the Lombardi era.

19. Johnny "Blood" McNally, HB, 1929–1933, 1935–1936: Played a major role in Green Bay's titles from 1929 to 1931 and the 1936 championship. McNally led the Packers in scoring in 1931 and 1932 and was named to the Hall of Fame in 1963.

20. Fred "Fuzzy" Thurston, G, 1959–1967: Green Bay's left guard during the "Glory Years." Thurston was an integral part of one of the most storied offensive lines in league history. He received All-Pro honors five seasons and was named to the Packers Hall of Fame in 1975.

21. Sterling Sharpe, WR, 1988–1994: Holds Green Bay's all-time reception mark with 595 career catches. His 112 receptions in 1993 and 108 in 1992 are the top two single-season marks in franchise history. Sharpe's career ended in the 1994 season after he suffered a spinal injury. He was named to the Packers Hall of Fame in 2002.

22. Bobby Dillon, FS, 1952–1959: Holder of the Packers' all-time record with 52 career interceptions. Dillon led Green Bay in picks each year from 1952 to 1958, including three seasons where he had nine interceptions. He also holds the team record with four interceptions in a game. He was named to the Packers Hall of Fame in 1974.

23. Gale Gillingham, G, 1966–1974, 1976: A first-round draft choice in 1966 and arguably the most dominant offensive lineman in the Lombardi era. Green Bay coach Dan Devine inexplicably moved Gillingham, a three-time Pro Bowl offensive guard, to defensive tackle in 1972, where he suffered a season-ending knee injury. Gillingham was named to the Packers Hall of Fame in 1982.

24. Ahman Green, RB, 2000–present: Set Packers' single-season record for rushing yards (1,833) and touchdowns (20) in 2003. Green ranks second in team history in career rushing yards (7,103), is tied with Jim Taylor for consecutive 1,000-yard seasons (five), and holds the team record for most rushing yards in a game (218 against Denver in 2003).

25. Boyd Dowler, WR, 1959–1969: Led Green Bay in receiving seven times. Dowler ranks fourth in team history in receptions (448) and fourth in receiving yards (6,918). He was inducted into the Packers Hall of Fame in 1978.

26. Max McGee, WR, 1954, 1957–1967: McGee's 50 touchdown receptions rank fourth in team history. McGee had a game to remember in Super Bowl I, catching seven passes for 138 yards and two touchdowns. He was named to the Packers Hall of Fame in 1975.

27. Cecil Isbell, WB/QB, 1938–1942: Ranks eighth in team history in touchdown passes (61), ninth in yards (5,945), and fifth in passer rating (72.6). Isbell did much of his damage hooking up with Don Hutson. He was inducted into the Packers Hall of Fame in 1972.

28. Paul Coffman, TE, 1978–1985: Ranks eighth in franchise history with 322 receptions and 10th in receiving yards (4,223). Coffman was named to three Pro Bowls and inducted into the team Hall of Fame in 1994.

29. LeRoy Butler, SS, 1990–2001: Ranks fourth in team history in career interceptions (38) and led the team in picks five times. Butler was a key member of the 1996 Super Bowl championship team, which had the league's number one–ranked defense.

30. Dave Robinson, LB, 1963–1972: Starting linebacker for nine years. Robinson helped the Packers win world championships from 1965 to 1967 and was named to the Packers Hall of Fame in 1982.

31. Mike Michalske, G, 1929–1935, 1937: One of the game's most dominant guards during the "two-way" era. A two-time All-Pro selection, Michalske earned the nickname "Iron Mike." He was elected to the Pro Football Hall of Fame in 1964.

32. Dave Hanner, DT, 1952–1964: Two-time Pro Bowl player whose 13 years as a Packer tie for fifth in number of years spent with the team. Hanner later worked as an assistant coach from 1965 to 1979 and again in 1982. He was inducted into the Packers Hall of Fame in 1974.

33. Arnie Herber, RB/QB, 1930–1940: Won NFL passing titles in 1932, 1934, and 1936 and teamed with Don Hutson to form the league's most dangerous passing duo in football in the midthirties. Herber ranks fifth in Packers history with 66 career touchdown passes. He was named to the Pro Football Hall of Fame in 1966.

34. Antonio Freeman, WR, 1995–2001, 2003: Ranks fifth in team history in receptions (431) and third in touchdown receptions (57). Freeman led the Packers in catches each season from 1996 to 1999 and set a record with his 81-yard touchdown reception in Super Bowl XXXI.

35. Lynn Dickey, QB, 1976–1977, 1979–1985: Ranks third in team history in career passing yards (21,369) and touchdown passes (133). Dickey holds the single-season record with 4,458 passing yards in 1983. He was inducted into the Packers Hall of Fame in 1992.

36. Donny Anderson, HB, 1966–1971: Led the team in rushing in 1968 and 1970. He was inducted into the Packers Hall of Fame in 1983.

37. Bill Howton, WR, 1952–1958: Led Packers in receptions and receiving yards for six consecutive seasons. Howton also led the NFL in receiving yards in 1952 and 1957. He was inducted into the Packers Hall of Fame in 1974.

38. Bill Forester, LB, 1953–1963: A college defensive tackle who reached four Pro Bowls and was named All-Pro five times as a Green Bay linebacker. Forester helped the Packers win world championships in 1961 and 1962.

39. Carroll Dale, WR, 1965–1972: Led Green Bay in receiving six times and was named to three Pro Bowls. Dale averaged 19.72 yards per catch, the most in team history. He was inducted into the Packers Hall of Fame in 1979.

40. Tobin Rote, QB, 1950–1956: Ranks fourth in career passing yards (11,535) and passing touchdowns (89). Rote threw more passes than any rookie quarterback in Packers history (224). He was inducted into the Packers Hall of Fame in 1974.

41. LaVern "Lavvie" Dilweg, E, 1927–1934: Key component in the Packers' three consecutive championship teams from 1929 to 1931. Dilweg scored 14 career touchdowns and was among the first class inducted into the Packers Hall of Fame in 1970.

42. Larry McCarren, C, 1973–1984: Played 162 consecutive games, fourth most in franchise history. McCarren was named to the Pro Bowl in

1982, named All-Pro in 1983, and inducted into the Packers Hall of Fame in 1992.

43. Willie Buchanon, DB, 1972–1978: Three-time Pro Bowl selection who had 21 interceptions in Green Bay, including four in a 1978 game against San Diego. Buchanon was traded to the Chargers after the 1978 season. He was inducted into the Packers Hall of Fame in 1993.

44. Larry Craig, E/B, 1939–1949: Two-time Pro Bowl selection who was also named All-Pro twice. Craig was inducted into the Packers Hall of Fame in 1973.

45. Ron Kramer, TE, 1957, 1959–1964: Named All-Pro twice and a Pro Bowl selection once. Kramer was inducted into the Packers Hall of Fame in 1975.

46. Fred Carr, LB, 1968–1977: Eight-year starter at outside linebacker. Carr was named to three Pro Bowls and was an All-Pro selection once. He was inducted into the Packers Hall of Fame in 1983.

47. Charles "Buckets" Goldenberg, G/B, 1933–1945: Named All-Pro twice and elected to one Pro Bowl. Goldenberg, part of the second class ever inducted into the Packers Hall of Fame (1972), was part of NFL championship teams in 1936, 1939, and 1944.

48. Ryan Longwell, K, 1997–2005: Green Bay's all-time leading scorer with 1,054 points. Longwell holds the team record for field goals (226) and extra points (376) and made a team-record 81.6 percent of his field-goal attempts.

49. Edgar Bennett, RB, 1992–1996: Ranks ninth in team history with 3,353 rushing yards. Bennett ran for 1,067 yards in 1995, becoming the first Packers running back in 17 years to eclipse the 1,000-yard barrier. He was the primary ball carrier on Green Bay's Super Bowl championship team in 1996 and was named to the Packers Hall of Fame in 2005.

50. Chris Jacke, K, 1989–1996: Ranks third on the team's all-time scoring list (820). Jacke led the Packers in scoring in seven of his eight seasons with the team and made 77.2 percent of his field-goal attempts.

By the NUMBERS 133—Number of people inducted into the Green Bay Packers Hall of Fame. The following is a list of players, coaches, general managers, etc., and the year they were inducted.

1970: Bernard "Boob" Darling, C, 1927–1931; Curly Lambeau, B-coach, 1919–1949; Lavvie Dilweg, E, 1927–1934; Verne Lewellen, B, 1924–1932; Jug Earp, C, 1922–1932; Johnny "Blood" McNally, B, 1929–1933, 1935–1936; Cal Hubbard, T, 1929–1933, 1935; Mike Michalske, G, 1929–1935, 1937.

1972: Hank Bruder, G, 1931–1939; Don Hutson, E-DB, 1935–1945; Milt Gantenbein, E, 1931–1940; Cecil Isbell, B, 1938–1942; Chas "Buckets" Goldenberg, G-B, 1933–1945; Joe Laws, B, 1934–1945; Arnie Herber, B, 1930–1940; Russ Letlow, G, 1936–1942, 1946; Clarke Hinkle, B, 1932–1941; George Svendsen, C-LB, 1935–1937, 1940–1941.

1973: Charley Brock, C-LB, 1939–1947; Bob Monnett, B, 1933–1938; Tony Canadeo, B, 1941–1944, 1946–1952; Buford "Baby" Ray, T, 1938–1948; Larry Craig, B-E, 1939–1949; Andy Uram, HB, 1938–1943; Bob Forte, B, 1946–1953; Dick Wildung, T, 1946–1951, 1953; Ted Fritsch, B, 1942–1950; H. L. "Whitey" Woodin, G, 1922–1931.

1974: Al Carmichael, RB-KR, 1953–1958; Dave Hanner, DT, 1952–1964; Fred Cone, FB-K, 1951–1957; Billy Howton, E, 1952–1958; Bobby Dillon, DB, 1952–1959; John Martinkovic, E, 1951–1956; Howie Ferguson, FB, 1953–1958; Jim Ringo, C, 1953–1963; Bill Forester, LB, 1953–1963; Tobin Rote, QB, 1950–1956.

1975: Don Chandler, K, 1965–1967; Ron Kramer, TE, 1957, 1959–1964; Willie Davis, DE, 1960–1969; Vince Lombardi, coach-GM, 1959–1968; Paul Hornung, HB-K, 1957–1962, 1964–1966; Max McGee, E, 1954, 1957–1967; Henry Jordan, DT, 1959–1969; Jim Taylor, FB, 1958–1966; Jerry Kramer, G, 1958–1968; Fred "Fuzzy" Thurston, G, 1959–1967.

1976: Joseph "Red" Dunn, B, 1927–1931; Bob Skoronski, T, 1956, 1959–1968; Hank Gremminger, DB, 1956–1965; Jesse Whittenton, DB, 1958–1964; Gary Knafelc, E, 1954–1962; Carl "Bud" Jorgensen, trainer, 1924–1970.

1977: Howard "Cub" Buck, T, 1921–1925; Bart Starr, QB, 1956–1971; Forrest Gregg, T, 1956, 1958–1970; Andrew B. Turnbull, president, 1923–1927; Charlie Mathys, B, 1922–1926; Willie Wood, S, 1960–1971.

1978: Boyd Dowler, WR, 1959–1969; Paul "Tiny" Engebretsen, G, 1934–1941; Lon Evans, G, 1933–1937; Ray Nitschke, LB, 1958–1972; George Calhoun, publicity director, 1919–1946.

1979: Nate Barragar, C, 1931–1932, 1934–1935; Carroll Dale, E, 1965–1972; Elijah Pitts, RB, 1961–1969, 1971; Pete Tinsley, G-LB, 1938–1939, 1941–1945; Dominic Olejniczak, president, 1958–1982.

1981: Herb Adderley, 1961–1969; Ken Bowman, C, 1964–1973; Chester "Swede" Johnston, 1931, 1934–1938; Lee H. Joannes, president, 1930–1947.

1982: Lou Brock, 1940–1945; Gale Gillingham, G, 1966–1974, 1976; Dave Robinson, LB, 1963–1972; Jack Vainisi, scout, 1950–1960.

1983: Donny Anderson, RB, 1966–1971; Fred Carr, LB, 1968–1977; Carl Mulleneaux, E, 1938–1941, 1945–1946; Fred Leicht, contributor.

1984: John Brockington, RB, 1971–1977; Dan Currie, LB, 1958–1964; Ed Jankowski, B, 1937–1941.

1985: Phil Bengtson, coach-GM, 1959–1970; Bob Jeter, DB, 1963–1970; Earl "Bud" Svendsen, C-LB, 1937, 1939.

1986: Lee Roy Caffey, LB, 1964–1969; Irv Comp, B, 1943–1949; Wilner Burke, contributor, 1938–1981.

1987: Chester Marcol, K, 1972–1980; Deral Teteak, LB-G, 1952–1956; Dr. E. S. Brusky, contributor, 1962–1990.

1988: Lionel Aldridge, DE, 1963–1971; Bob Mann, E, 1950–1954; Jerry Atkinson, contributor.

1989: Zeke Bratkowski, QB, 1963–1968, 1971; Ron Kostelnik, DT, 1961–1968.

1991: Harry Jacunski, E, 1939–1944; Jan Stenerud, K, 1980–1983; Gerald L. Clifford, contributor.

1992: Lynn Dickey, QB, 1976–1977, 1979–1985; Larry McCarren, C, 1973–1984; Al Schneider, contributor.

1993: Willie Buchanon, CB, 1972–1978; Johnnie Gray, S, 1975–1983; Art Daley, contributor.

1994: Paul Coffman, TE, 1978–1985; Gerry Ellis, FB, 1980–1986; Dr. W. Webber Kelly, contributor.

1995: William Brault, HOF founder.

1996: John Anderson, LB, 1978–1989; Lee Remmel, contributor.

1997: John "Red" Cochran, coach-scout, 1959–1966, 1971–2004; Ezra Johnson, DE, 1977–1987; Travis Williams, RB-KR, 1967–1970.

1998: Ken Ellis, CB, 1970–1975; Mark Murphy, S, 1980–1985, 1987–1991; Robert J. Parins, president, 1982–1989.

1999: James Lofton, WR, 1978–1986; Tim Miller, contributor, 1956–1988.

2000: Ron Wolf, executive VP-GM, 1991–2001.

2001: Johnny Holland, LB, 1987–1993; Ray Scott, contributor.

2002: Sterling Sharpe, WR, 1988–1994; Vernon Biever, contributor.

2003: Mike Douglass, LB, 1978–1985; Jim Irwin, contributor.

2004: Bob Harlan, president-CEO, 1989–present.

2005: Don Majkowski, QB, 1987–1992; Edgar Bennett, RB, 1992–1996.

2006: Reggie White, DE, 1993–1998.

ANSWERS TO
TRIVIA QUESTIONS

Page 5: Minnesota broke Green Bay's 25-game home winning streak in 1998 by a score of 37–24.

Page 7: Green Bay scored its most points in a 41–16 win over the St. Louis Cardinals in the first round of the 1982 playoffs.

Page 11: Yes, Green Bay has posted two post-season shutouts. One was a 27–0 win over the New York Giants in the 1939 NFL championship and the other a 37–0 win over the New York Giants in the 1961 NFL championship.

Page 19: Jim McMahon was on Green Bay's roster during its 1996 Super Bowl season.

Page 23: Tyrone Williams won an NCAA championship with Nebraska the year prior to Green Bay's winning the 1996 Super Bowl.

Page 30: Green Bay drafted Torrance Marshall from Oklahoma in 2001, Najeh Davenport from Miami in 2002, and Kenny Peterson from Ohio State in 2003.

Page 33: Bart Starr was selected in the 17th round of the 1956 draft.

Page 37: C. The current capacity of Lambeau Field is 72,601.

Page 41: The Packers began playing games at Lambeau Field in 1957.

Page 52: Green Bay has selected the most players (41) from Minnesota.

Page 56: D. Mike Michalske, a guard who played with the Packers from 1929 to 1935 and again in 1937, has worn the most uniform numbers (nine) in his career.

Page 60: The first Packer to eclipse 1,000 yards rushing in a single season was Tony Canadeo in 1949.

Page 65: C. Earl "Curly" Lambeau coached Green Bay for 29 years, from 1921 to 1949.

Page 69: The only Packers coach to have exactly a .500 career winning percentage in Green Bay was Ray Rhodes, who went 8–8 in 1999.

Page 72: A. Vince Lombardi attended Fordham.

Page 77: Don Hutson and Bart Starr both attended Alabama.

Page 81: The Green Bay Packers have 111,921 stockholders; the group holds 4,749,925 shares, and no member of the group receives a dividend.

Page 85: C. Green Bay earned its first-ever win against the Minneapolis Marines, 7–6, on October 23, 1921, at Green Bay's Hagemeister Park.

Page 88: The Chicago Bears have the most players (26) in the Pro Football Hall of Fame.

Page 92: The Packers' won-loss record for postseason play through 2005 is 24–14.

Page 95: No franchise has more NFL championships than Green Bay has. Chicago is second with nine.

Page 101: True. Green Bay was the first team ever to fly to a road game, which they did in 1938, splitting the squad into two groups so the entire team wouldn't be wiped out in the case of a plane crash.

Page 103: Mark Chmura caught Brett Favre's two-point-conversion pass in Super Bowl XXXI.

Page 111: Bobby Dillon holds the Packers' career record for interceptions, with 52.

Page 115: Brett Favre and Antonio Freeman combined for 57 touchdowns.

Page 117: Green Bay surrendered five draft picks—two first-round, one second, and two thirds—to the Los Angeles Rams for quarterback John Hadl.

Page 125: Five Packers have had their numbers retired; they are Tony Canadeo (No. 3), Don Hutson (No. 14), Bart Starr (No. 15), Ray Nitschke (No. 66), and Reggie White (No. 92).

Page 131: Through 2005, Forrest Gregg had been named to the most Pro Bowls (nine). Brett Favre and Willie Wood were tied for second with eight each.

Page 136: A. Tony Canadeo's nickname was "Grey Ghost."

Page 138: Ryan Longwell is Green Bay's all-time leading scorer; he has 1,054 career points.

Page 142: In addition to Lambeau Field, Green Bay has called seven other fields home; they are Hagemeister Park (1919–1922), Bellevue Park (1923–1924), and City Stadium (1925–1956) in Green Bay and Borchert Field (1933), State Fair Park (1934–1951), Marquette Stadium (1952), and County Stadium (1953–1994) in Milwaukee.

Page 151: Don Hutson has the most touchdowns in Packers history, with 105.

Green Bay Packers All-Time Roster (through 2005 season)

Players on this roster have appeared in at least one regular-season or playoff game with the Packers.

A

Cliff Aberson (B), No College	1946
Nate Abrams (E), No College	1921
George Abramson (G-T), Minnesota	1925
Ron Acks (LB), Illinois	1974–1976
Chet Adams (T), Ohio State	1943
Herb Adderley (DB), Michigan State	1961–1969
Bob Adkins (B), Marshall	1940–1941, 1945
Erik Affholter (WR), USC	1991
Dick Afflis (G), Nevada	1951–1954
Ben Agajanian (K), New Mexico	1961
Louie Aguiar (P), Utah State	1999
Chris Akins (S), Arkansas–Pine Bluff	2000–2001
Art Albrecht (T), Wisconsin	1942
Ben Aldridge (B), Oklahoma A&M	1953
Lionel Aldridge (DE), Utah State	1963–1971
Kurt Allerman (LB), Penn State	1980–1981
Marty Amsler (DE), Evansville	1970
Norm Amundsen (G), Wisconsin	1957
Aric Anderson (LB), Millikin	1987
Bill Anderson (TE), Tennessee	1965–1966
Donny Anderson (RB), Texas Tech	1966–1971
John Anderson (LB), Michigan	1978–1989
Marques Anderson (S), UCLA	2002–2003
Vickey Ray Anderson (FB), Oklahoma	1980
Joe Andruzzi (G), Southern Connecticut State	1998–1999
Charlie Ane (C), Michigan State	1981
Marger Apsit (B), USC	1932
Lester Archambeau (DE), Stanford	1990–1992
Billy Ard (G-T), Wake Forest	1989–1991
Mike Ariey (T), San Diego State	1989
Jahine Arnold (WR), Fresno State	1999
Mike Arthur (C), Texas A&M	1995–1996
Rodney Artmore (C), Baylor	1999
Roger Ashmore (T), Gonzaga	1928–1929
Bert Askson (TE), Texas Southern	1975–1977
Steve Atkins (RB), Maryland	1971–1981
Todd Auer (LB), Western Illinois	1989
Hise Austin (DB), Prairie View A&M	1973
Steve Avery (FB), Northern Michigan	1991
Buddy Aydelette (G), Alabama	1980

B

Byron Bailey (HB), Washington State	1953
Karsten Bailey (WR), Auburn	2002–2003
Bill Bain (T), USC	1975
Frank Baker (E), Northwestern	1931
Roy Baker (B), USC	1928–1929
Frank Balazs (B), Iowa	1939–1941
Al Baldwin (E), Arkansas	1950
Herb Banet (B), Manchester	1937
Bob Barber (DE), Grambling State	1976–1979
Bryan Barker (P), Santa Clara	2004
Roy Barker (DE), North Carolina	1999
Emery Barnes (DE), Oregon	1956
Gary Barnes (E), Clemson	1962
Nick Barnett (LB), Oregon State	2003–2005
Solon Barnett (T), Baylor	1945–1946
Nate Barragar (C), USC	1931–1932, 1934–1935
Jan Barrett (E), Fresno State	1963
Sebastian Barrie (DE), Liberty	1992
Al Barry (G), USC	1954, 1957
Kevin Barry (T), Arizona	2002–2005
Norm Barry (B), Notre Dame	1921
Don Barton (B), Texas	1953
Mike Bartrum (TE), Marshall	1995

Carl Barzilauskas (DT), Indiana	1978–1979	Nate Borden (DE), Indiana	1955–1959
Myrt Basing (B), Lawrence	1923–1927	Dirk Borgognone (K), Pacific	1995
Mike Basinger (DE), Cal–Riverside	1974	Jim Bowdoin (G), Alabama	1928–1931
Lloyd Baxter (C), SMU	1948	Matt Bowen (S), Iowa	2001–2002
Sanjay Beach (WR), Colorado State	1992	David Bowens (DE), Western Illinois	2000
Jack Beasey (B), South Dakota	1924	Ken Bowman (C), Wisconsin	1964–1973
Ken Beck (DT), Texas A&M	1959–1960	Jerry Boyarsky (NT), Pittsburgh	1986–1989
Wayland Becker (E), Marquette	1936–1938	Elmo Boyd (WR), Western Kentucky	1978
Brad Bedell (G-T), Colorado	2004	Greg Boyd (DE), San Diego State	1983
Don Beebe (WR), Chadron State	1996–1997	Don Bracken (P), Michigan	1985–1990
Bruce Beekley (LB), Oregon	1980	Charlie Brackins (QB), Prairie View A&M	1955
Albert Bell (WR), Alabama	1988	Corey Bradford (WR), Jackson State	1998–2001
Ed Bell (G-T), Indiana	1947–1949	Dave Bradley (G), Penn State	1969–1971
Tyrone Bell (CB), North Alabama	1999	Jeff Brady (LB), Kentucky	1992
Earl Bennett (G), Hardin-Simmons	1946	Byron Braggs (DE), Alabama	1981–1983
Edgar Bennett (RB), Florida State	1992–1996	Kent Branstetter (T), Houston	1973
Tony Bennett (LB), Mississippi	1990–1993	Zeke Bratkowski (QB), Georgia	1963–1968, 1971
Paul Berezney (T), Fordham	1942–1944	Ray Bray (G), Western Michigan	1952
Ed Berrang (E), Villanova	1952	Gene Breen (LB), Virginia Tech	1964
Connie Berry (E), North Carolina State	1940	Jack Brennan (G), Michigan	1939
Ed Berry (DB), Utah State	1986	Charley Brock (C-LB), Nebraska	1939–1947
Gary Berry (S), Ohio State	2000	Lou Brock (B), Purdue	1940–1945
Larry Bettencourt (C), St. Mary's (California)	1933	Matt Brock (DE-DT), Michigan	1989–1994
Tom Bettis (LB), Purdue	1955–1961	John Brockington (RB), Ohio State	1971–1977
David Beverley (P), Auburn	1975–1980	Barrett Brooks (T), Kansas State	2002
Josh Bidwell (P), Oregon	2000–2003	Bucky Brooks (CB), North Carolina	1996–1997
Adolph Bieberstein (G), Wisconsin	1926	Robert Brooks (WR), South Carolina	1992–1998
Atari Bigby (S), Central Florida	2005	Mal Bross (B), Gonzaga	1927
Dick Bilda (B), Marquette	1944	Steve Broussard (P), Southern Mississippi	1975
Lewis Billups (CB), North Alabama	1992	Aaron Brown (DE), Minnesota	1973–1974
John Biolo (G), Lake Forest	1939	Allen Brown (TE), Mississippi	1966–1967
Tom Birney (K), Michigan State	1979–1980	Bob Brown (DT), Arkansas AM&N	1966–1973
Roosevelt Blackmon (CB), Morris Brown	1998	Buddy Brown (G), Arkansas	1953–1956
Jeff Blackshear (G), Northeast Louisiana	2002	Carlos Brown (QB), Pacific	1975–1976
Ed Blaine (G), Missouri	1962	Dave Brown (CB), Michigan	1987–1989
Michael Blair (RB), Ball State	1998	Gary Brown (T), Georgia Tech	1994–1996
Carl Bland (WR), Virginia Union	1989–1990	Gilbert Brown (DT), Kansas	1993–1999,
Elbert Bloodgood (B), Nebraska	1930		2000–2003
Bill Boedeker (B), Kalamazoo	1950	Jonathan Brown (DE), Tennessee	1998
Chuck Boerio (LB), Illinois	1952	Ken Brown (C), New Mexico	1980
Juran Bolden (CB), Mississippi Delta	1998	Robert Brown (LB-DE), Virginia Tech	1982–1992
Scott Bolton (WR), Auburn	1988	Tim Brown (HB), Ball State	1959
Warren Bone (DE), Texas Southern	1987	Tom Brown (DB), Maryland	1964–1968
Steve Bono (QB), UCLA	1997	Ross Browner (DE-NT), Notre Dame	1987
Vaughn Booker (DE-DT), Cincinnati	1998–1999	Hank Bruder (B), Northwestern	1931–1939
Billy Bookout (DB), Austin	1955–1956	Mark Brunell (QB), Washington	1993–1994
J. R. Boone (B), Tulsa	1953	Mike Buccianeri (G), Indiana	1941, 1944–1945
Fritz Borak (E), Creighton	1938	Willie Buchanon (CB), San Diego State	1972–1978

Cub Buck (T), Wisconsin	1921–1925	Don Chandler (K), Florida	1965–1967
Terrell Buckley (CB), Florida State	1992–1994	Antonio Chatman (WR-KR), Cincinnati	2003–2005
Larry Buhler (B), Minnesota	1939–1941	Louis Cheek (T), Texas A&M	1991
Walt Buland (T), No College	1924	Bill Cherry (C), Middle Tennessee State	1986–1987
Hank Bullough (G), Michigan State	1955–1958	Francis Chesley (LB), Wyoming	1978
Ronnie Burgess (DB), Wake Forest	1985	Henry Childs (TE), Kansas State	1984
Reggie Burnette (LB), Houston	1991	Mark Chmura (TE), Boston College	1993–1999
Paul Burris (G), Oklahoma	1949–1951	Putt Choate (LB), SMU	1987
Curtis Burrow (K), Central Arkansas	1988	Paul Christman (QB), Missouri	1950
Jim Burrow (DB), Nebraska	1976	Gus Cifelli (T), Notre Dame	1953
Blair Bush (C), Washington	1989–1991	Bob Cifers (B), Tennessee	1949
Bill Butler (B), Chattanooga	1959	Jack Clancy (WR), Michigan	1970
Frank Butler (C-T), Michigan State	1934–1936, 1938	Chuck Clanton (DB), Auburn	1985
LeRoy Butler (CB-S), Florida State	1990–2001	Dennis Claridge (QB), Nebraska	1965
Mike Butler (DE), Kansas	1977–1982, 1985	Allan Clark (RB), Northern Arizona	1982
Art Buttman (C), Marquette	1932–1934	Greg Clark (LB), Arizona State	1991
		Jessie Clark (FB), Arkansas	1983–1987
C		Vinnie Clark (CB), Ohio State	1991–1992
Brian Cabral (LB), Colorado	1980	Shannon Clavelle (DE), Colorado	1995–1997
Mossy Cade (DB), Texas	1985–1986	Mark Clayton (WR), Louisville	1993
Lee Roy Caffey (LB), Texas A&M	1964–1969	Bob Clemens (FB), Georgia	1955
Ivan Cahoon (T), Gonzaga	1926–1929	Cal Clemens (B), USC	1936
David Caldwell (NT), TCU	1987	Ray Clemens (G), St. Mary's (California)	1947
Rich Campbell (QB), California	1981–1984	Chad Clifton (T), Tennessee	2000–2005
James Campen (C), Tulane	1989–1993	Jack Cloud (FB), William & Mary	1950–1951
Tony Canadeo (B), Gonzaga	1941–1944, 1946–1952	Reggie Cobb (RB), Tennessee	1994
		Ed Cody (B), Purdue	1947–1948
Al Cannava (B), Boston College	1950	Junior Coffey (RB), Washington	1965
Mark Cannon (C), Texas-Arlington	1984–1989	Paul Coffman (TE), Kansas State	1978–1985
Dick Capp (TE-LB), Boston College	1967	Keo Coleman (LB), Mississippi State	1993
Jim Capuzzi (B), Cincinnati	1955–1956	Colin Cole (DT), Iowa	2004–2005
Joe Carey (G), Illinois Tech	1921	Steve Collier (T), Bethune-Cookman	1987
Wes Carlson (G), St. John's	1926	Albin Collins (HB), LSU	1951
Al Carmichael (HB), USC	1953–1958	Bobby Collins (TE), North Alabama	2001
Lew Carpenter (B), Arkansas	1959–1963	Brett Collins (LB), Washington	1992–1993
Fred Carr (LB), Texas–El Paso	1968–1977	Mark Collins (CB), Cal State–Fullerton	1997
Alphonso Carreker (DE), Florida State	1984–1988	Nick Collins (S), Bethune-Cookman	2005
Ahmad Carroll (CB), Arkansas	2004–2005	Patrick Collins (RB), Oklahoma	1998
Leo Carroll (DE), San Diego State	1968	Shawn Collins (WR), Northern Arizona	1993
Paul Ott Carruth (RB), Alabama	1986–1988	Derek Combs (CB), Ohio State	2003
Carl Carter (CB), Texas Tech	1992	Irv Comp (B), St. Benedict	1943–1949
Jim Carter (LB), Minnesota	1970–1975, 1977–1978	Chuck Compton (DB), Boise State	1987
Joe Carter (E), SMU	1942	Rudy Comstock (G), Georgetown	1931–1933
Mike Carter (WR), Sacramento State	1970	Jack Concannon (QB), Boston College	1974
Tony Carter (FB), Minnesota	2002	Fred Cone (FB-K), Clemson	1951–1957
Charley Casper (B), TCU	1934	Dave Conway (K), Texas	1971
Ron Cassidy (WR), Utah State	1979–1981, 1983–1984	James Cook (G), Notre Dame	1921
Chuck Cecil (S), Arizona	1988–1992	Kelly Cook (RB), Oklahoma State	1987

Ted Cook (E-DB), Alabama	1948–1950
Bill Cooke (DE), Massachusetts	1975
Kerry Cooks (S), Iowa	1998
Mark Cooney (LB), Colorado	1974
Russell Copeland (WR), Memphis State	1998
John Corker (LB), Oklahoma State	1988
Junius Coston (G-T), North Carolina A&T	2005
Frank Coughlin (T), Notre Dame	1921
Larry Coutre (HB), Notre Dame	1950, 1953
Ron Cox (LB), Fresno State	1996
Larry Craig (E-B), Alabama	1948–1950
Keith Crawford (CB-WR), Howard Payne	1995, 1999
Ted Cremer (E), Auburn	1948
Leon Crenshaw (DT), Tuskegee	1968
Bernie Crimmons (G-B), Notre Dame	1945
Milburn Croft (T), Ripon	1942–1947
Tommy Cronin (HB), Marquette	1922
Dave Croston (T), Iowa	1988
Ray Crouse (RB), Nevada–Las Vegas	1984
Jim Crowley (HB), Notre Dame	1925
Tommy Crutcher (LB), TCU	1964–1967, 1971–1972
Ward Cuff (B), Marquette	1947
Jim Culbreath (FB), Oklahoma	1977–1979
Al Culver (T), Notre Dame	1932
George Cumby (LB), Oklahoma	1980–1985
Mike Curcio (LB), Temple	1983
Dan Currie (LB), Michigan State	1958–1964
Bill Curry (C), Georgia Tech	1965–1966
Scott Curry (T), Montana	1999
Andy Cverko (G), Northwestern	1960
Hector Cyre (T), Gonzaga	1926

D

Tom Dahms (T), San Diego State	1955
Carroll Dale (WR), Virginia Tech	1965–1972
Joe Danelo (K), Washington State	1975
Averell Daniell (T), Pittsburgh	1937
Ernie Danjean (LB), Auburn	1957
Chris Darkins (RB), Minnesota	1997
Bernard Darling (C), Beloit	1927–1931
Bill Davenport (HB), Hardin-Simmons	1931
Najeh Davenport (RB-FB), Miami (Florida)	2002–2005
Don Davey (DE-DT), Wisconsin	1991–1994
Ben Davidson (DE), Washington	1961
Anthony Davis (LB), Utah	1999
Dave Davis (WR), Tennessee A&I	1971–1972
Harper Davis (B), Mississippi State	1951

Kenneth Davis (RB), TCU	1986–1988
Paul Davis (G), Marquette	1922
Ralph Davis (G), Wisconsin	1947–1948
Rob Davis (LS), Shippensburg	1997–2005
Tyrone Davis (TE), Virginia	1997–2002
Willie Davis (DE), Grambling State	1960–1969
Dale Dawson (K), Eastern Kentucky	1988
Gib Dawson (HB), Texas	1953
Walter Dean (FB), Grambling State	1991
Don Deeks (T), Texas	1948
Bob Dees (T), Southwest Missouri State	1952
Tony Degrate (DE), Texas	1985
Jim Del Gaizo (QB), Tampa	1973
Al Del Greco (K), Auburn	1984–1987
Jim DeLisle (DT), Wisconsin	1971
Jeff Dellenbach (C-G)	1996–1998
Tony DeLuca (NT), Rhode Island	1984
Patrick Dendy (CB), Rice	2005
Preston Dennard (WR), New Mexico	1985
Burnell Dent (LB), Tulane	1986–1992
Dick Deschaine (P), No College	1955–1957
Ty Detmer (QB), BYU	1992–1995
Lynn Dickey (QB), Kansas State	1976–1977, 1979–1985
Clint Didier (TE), Portland State	1988–1989
Na'il Diggs (LB), Ohio State	2000–2005
Bobby Dillon (DB), Texas	1952–1959
Anthony Dilweg (QB), Duke	1989–1990
Lavvie Dilweg (E), Marquette	1927–1934
Rich Dimler (DT), USC	1980
Antonio Dingle (DT), Virginia	1999
Ray DiPierro (G), Ohio State	1950–1951
Leo Disend (T), Albright	1940
John Dittrich (G), Wisconsin	1959
Waldo Don Carlos (C), Drake	1931
Mark D'Onofrio (LB), Penn State	1992
Mike Donohoe (TE), San Francisco	1973–1974
Matthew Dorsett (CB), Southern	1995
Dean Dorsey (K), Toronto	1988
John Dorsey (LB), Connecticut	1984–1988
Earl Dotson (T), Texas A&I	1993–2002
Santana Dotson (DT), Baylor	1996–2001
George Douglas (C), Marquette	1921
Bobby Douglass (QB), Kansas	1978
Mike Douglass (LB), San Diego State	1978–1985
Corey Dowden (CB), Tulane	1996
Steve Dowden (T), Baylor	1952
Boyd Dowler (WR), Colorado	1959–1969
Brian Dowling (QB), Yale	1977

Dave Drechsler (G), North Carolina	1983–1984
Wally Dreyer (B), Wisconsin	1950
Donald Driver (WR), Alcorn State	1999–2005
Jeff Drost (DT), Iowa	1977
Chuck Drulis (G), Temple	1950
Forey Duckett (CB), Nevada-Reno	1994
Wilfred Duford (B), Marquette	1924
Paul Duhart (B), Florida	1944
Jamie Dukes (C), Florida State	1994
Bill DuMoe (E), No College	1921
Dave Dunaway (WR), Duke	1968
Ken Duncan (P), Tulsa	1971
Red Dunn (B), Marquette	1927–1931
Pat Dunnigan (E), Minnesota	1922

E

Ralph Earhart (B), Texas Tech	1948–1949
Jug Earp (C), Monmouth	1922–1932
Roger Eason (G), Oklahoma	1949
Ed Ecker (T), John Carroll	1950–1951
Antuan Edwards (CB-S), Clemson	1999–2003
Earl Edwards (DT), Wichita State	1979
Gary Ellerson (FB), Wisconsin	1985–1986
Burton Elliott (B), Marquette	1921
Carlton Elliott (E), Virginia	1951–1954
Tony Elliott (DB), Central Michigan	1987–1988
Gerry Ellis (FB), Missouri	1980–1986
Ken Ellis (CB), Southern	1970–1975
Dick Enderle (G), Minnesota	1976
Paul Engebretsen (G), Northwestern	1934–1941
Wuert Engelmann (B), South Dakota State	1930–1933
Rex Enright (FB), Notre Dame	1926–1927
Phillip Epps (WR), TCU	1982–1988
Mike Estep (G), Bowling Green	1987
Joe Ethridge (T), SMU	1949
Dick Evans (E), Iowa	1940, 1943
Doug Evans (CB), Louisiana Tech	1993–1997
Jack Evans (B), California	1929
Lon Evans (G), TCU	1933–1937

F

Tony Falkenstein (FB), St. Mary's (California)	1943
Mike Fanucci (DE), Arizona State	1974
Hal Faverty (C-LB), Wisconsin	1952
Brett Favre (QB), Southern Mississippi	1992–2005
Allen Faye (E), Marquette	1922
Greg Feasel (T), Abilene Christian	1986
Beattie Feathers (B), Tennessee	1940

Howie Ferguson (FB), No College	1953–1958
Robert Ferguson (WR), Texas A&M	2001–2005
Vince Ferragamo (QB), Nebraska	1985–1986
Bill Ferrario (G), Wisconsin	2002
Lou Ferry (T), Villanova	1949
Angelo Fields (T), Michigan State	1982
Tom Finnin (T), Detroit	1957
Tony Fisher (RB), Notre Dame	2002–2005
Kevin Fitzgerald (TE), Wisconsin–Eau Claire	1987
Paul Fitzgibbons (B), Creighton	1930–1932
Dick Flaherty (E), Marquette	1926
Mike Flanagan (C-T), UCLA	1998–2005
Jim Flanagan (LB), Pittsburgh	1967–1970
Jim Flanigan (DT), Notre Dame	2001
Marv Fleming (TE), Miami	1963–1969
Ryan Flinn (P), Central Florida	2005
Bob Flowers (C-LB), Texas Tech	1942–1949
Bobby Jack Floyd (FB), TCU	1952
Tom Flynn (S), Pittsburgh	1984–1986
Lee Folkins (DE), Washington	1961
Herman Fontenot (RB), LSU	1989–1990
Therrian Fontenot (CB), Fresno State	2005
Len Ford (DE), Michigan	1958
Bill Forester (LB), SMU	1953–1963
Aldo Forte (G), Montana	1947
Bob Forte (B), Arkansas	1946–1953
Joe Francis (B), Oregon State	1958–1959
Ray Frankowski (G), Washington	1945
Bubba Franks (TE), Miami (Florida)	2000–2005
Herb Franta (T), St. Thomas	1930
Nolan Franz (WR), Tulane	1986
Todd Franz (S), Tulsa	2002, 2005
Paul Frase (DE), Syracuse	1997
Antonio Freeman (WR), Virginia Tech	1995–2001, 2003
Bob Freeman (DB), Auburn	1959
Sherwood Fries (G-LB), Colorado State	1943
Ted Fritsch (B), Stevens Point Teachers	1942–1950
Ed Frutig (E), Michigan	1941–1945
Curtis Fuller (S), TCU	2003–2004
Joe Fuller (CB), Northern Iowa	1991
Brent Fullwood (RB), Auburn	1987–1990
Chuck Fusina (QB), Penn State	1986

G

Steve Gabbard (T), Florida State	1991
Samkon Gado (RB), Liberty	2005
Scott Galbraith (TE), USC	1998
Harry Galbreath (G), Tennessee	1993

Milt Gantenbein (E), Wisconsin	1931–1940
Eddie Garcia (K), SMU	1983–1984
Gus Gardella (RB), No College	1922
Milton Gardner (G), Wisconsin	1922–1926
Rod Gardner (WR), Clemson	2005
Bob Garrett (QB), Stanford	1954
Len Garrett (TE), New Mexico Highlands	1971–1973
Ron Gassert (DT), Virginia	1962
Lester Gatewood (C), Baylor	1946–1947
Buck Gavin (B), No College	1921, 1923
Kent Gaydos (WR), Florida State	1975
Kabeer Gbaja-Biamila, (DE) San Diego State	2000–2005
Charlie Getty (T), Penn State	1983
Jim Gillette (B), Virginia	1947
Gale Gillingham (G), Minnesota	1964–1974, 1976
Willie Gillus (QB), Norfolk State	1987
Jug Girad (B), Wisconsin	1948–1951
Chris Gizzi (LB), Air Force	2000–2001
Leland Glass (WR), Oregon	1972–1973
Terry Glenn (WR), Ohio State	2002
Eddie Glick (B), Marquette	1921–1922
Derrel Gofourth (G-C), Oklahoma State	1977–1982
Charles Goldenberg (G-B), Wisconsin	1933–1945
Herbert Goodman (RB), Graceland	2000–2001
Les Goodman (RB), Yankton	1973–1974
Clyde Goodnight (E), Tulsa	1945–1949
Darrien Gordon (CB-KR), Stanford	2002
Dick Gordon (WR), Michigan State	1973
Lou Gordon (T), Illinois	1936–1937
Ken Gorgal (DB), Purdue	1956
Jim Grabowski (RB), Illinois	1966–1970
Jay Graham (RB), Tennessee	2002
David Grant (DE), West Virginia	1973
Cecil Gray (T), North Carolina	1972
Jack Gray (E), No College	1923
Johnnie Gray (S), Cal State–Fullerton	1975–1983
Ahman Green (RB), Nebraska	2000–2005
Jessie Green (WR), Tulsa	1976
Tiger Green (S), Western Carolina	1986–1990
Norm Greeney (G), Notre Dame	1933
Tom Greenfield (C-LB), Arizona	1939–1941
David Greenwood (S), Wisconsin	1986
Forrest Gregg (T), SMU	1956, 1958–1970
Hank Gremminger (DB), Baylor	1956–1965
Harold Griffen (C), Iowa	1928
Billy Grimes (HB), Oklahoma A&M	1950–1952
Dan Grimm (G), Colorado	1963–1965

Earl Gros (FB), LSU	1962–1963
Roger Grove (B), Michigan State	1931–1935
Bob Gruber (T), Pittsburgh	1987
Jim Gueno (LB), Tulane	1976–1980

H

Dale Hackbart (DB), Wisconsin	1960–1961
Joey Hackett (TE), Elon	1987–1988
Michael Haddix (FB), Mississippi State	1989–1990
John Hadl (QB), Kansas	1974–1975
Darryl Haley (T), Utah	1988
Charlie Hall (CB), Pittsburgh	1971–1976
Lamont Hall (TE), Clemson	1999
Mark Hall (DE), Southwestern Louisiana	1989–1990
Ron Hallstrom (G), Iowa	1982–1992
Ruffin Hamilton (LB), Tulane	1994
Dave Hampton (RB), Wyoming	1969–1971
Dave Hanner (DT), Arkansas	1952–1964
Frank Hanny (T), Indiana	1930
Don Hansen (LB), Illinois	1976–1977
Hal Hansen (FB-E), Minnesota	1923
Chris Hanson (P), Marshall	1999
Derrick Harden (WR), Eastern New Mexico	1987
Leon Harden (S), Texas–El Paso	1970
Roger Harding (C), California	1949
Kevin Hardy (DT), Notre Dame	1970
James Hargrove (RB), Wake Forest	1987
Willard Harrell (RB), Pacific	1975–1977
Al Harris (CB), Texas A&M–Kingsville	2003–2005
Bernardo Harris (LB), North Carolina	1995–2001
Corey Harris (WR-CB-KR), Vanderbilt	1992–1994
Jack Harris (B), Wisconsin	1925–1926
Jackie Harris (TE), Northeast Louisiana	1990–1993
Leotis Harris (G), Arkansas	1978–1983
Raymont Harris (RB), Ohio State	1998
Tim Harris (LB), Memphis State	1986–1990
William Harris (TE), Bishop	1990
Anthony Harrison (DB), Georgia Tech	1987
Doug Hart (DB), Texas-Arlington	1964–1971
Perry Hartnett (G), SMU	1987
Keith Hartwig (WR), Arizona	1977
Maurice Harvey (S), Ball State	1981–1983
Matt Hasselbeck (QB), Boston College	1999–2000
Dave Hathcock (DB), Memphis State	1966
Tim Hauck (S), Montana	1991–1994
Dennis Havig (G), Colorado	1977
Mike Hawkins (CB), Oklahoma	2005
Michael Hawthorne (CB-S), Purdue	2003–2004

Ken Haycraft (E), Minnesota	1930
Aaron Hayden (RB), Tennessee	1997
Chris Hayes (S), Washington State	1996
Dave Hayes (E), Notre Dame	1921–1922
Gary Hayes (DB), Fresno State	1984–1986
Norb Hayes (E), Marquette	1923
Bill Hayhoe (T), USC	1969–1973
George Hays (DE), St. Bonaventure	1953
Les Hearden (HB), St. Ambrose	1924
Tom Hearden (B), Notre Dame	1927–1928
Stan Heath (QB), Nevada	1949
Larry Hefner (LB), Clemson	1972–1975
Craig Heimberger (G), Missouri	1999
Paul Held (QB), San Jose State	1955
Jerry Helluin (DT), Tulane	1954–1957
William Henderson (FB), North Carolina	1995–2005
Dutch Hendrian (B), Princeton	1924
Ted Hendricks (LB), Miami (Florida)	1974
Urban Henry (DT), Georgia Tech	1963
Craig Hentrich (P), Notre Dame	1994–1997
Arnie Herber (B), Regis	1930–1940
Noah Herron (RB), Northwestern	2005
Larry Hickman (FB), Baylor	1960
Don Highsmith (RB), Michigan State	1973
Don Hill (B), Stanford	1928
Jim Hill (DB), Texas A&I	1972–1974
Nate Hill (DE), Auburn	1988
John Hilton (TE), Richmond	1970
Dick Himes (T), Ohio State	1968–1977
Clarke Hinkle (FB), Bucknell	1932–1941
Hal Hinte (E), Pittsburgh	1942
Jim Hobbins (G), Minnesota	1987
Gary Hoffman (T), Santa Clara	1984
Darius Holland (DT-DE), Colorado	1995–1997
Johnny Holland (LB), Texas A&M	1987–1993
Ed Holler (LB), South Carolina	1963
Vonnie Holliday (DE), North Carolina	1998–2002
Lamont Hollinquest (LB), USC	1996–1998
Rob Holmberg (LB), Penn State	2001
Darick Holmes (RB), Portland State	1998
Jerry Holmes (CB), West Virginia	1990–1991
Estus Hood (DB), Illinois State	1978–1984
Charles Hope (G), Central (Ohio) State	1994
Don Horn (QB), San Diego State	1967–1970
Paul Hornung (B), Notre Dame	1957–1962, 1964–1966
Jason Horton (CB), North Carolina A&T	2004–2005
Bobby Houston (LB), North Carolina State	1990

Desmond Howard (WR-KR), Michigan	1996, 1999
Lynn Howard (B), Indiana	1921–1922
John Howell (B), Nebraska	1938
Billy Howton (E), Rice	1952–1958
Cal Hubbard (T), Cenetary, Geneva	1929–1933, 1935
Harlan Huckleby (RB), Michigan	1980–1985
Bob Hudson (RB), Northeastern (Oklahoma) State	1972
Tim Huffman (G-T), Notre Dame	1981–1985
Tom Hull (LB), Penn State	1975
Donnie Humphrey (DE), Auburn	1984–1986
Troy Humphrey (TE), Central Michigan	2005
Cletidus Hunt (DE-DT), Kentucky State	1999–2004
Ervin Hunt (DB), Fresno State	1970
Kevin Hunt (T), Doane	1972
Mike Hunt (LB), Minnesota	1978–1990
Art Hunter (C), Notre Dame	1954
Scott Hunter (QB), Alabama	1971–1973
Tony Hunter (RB), Minnesota	1987
Paul Hutchins (T), Western Michigan	1993–1994
Don Hutson (E-DB), Alabama	1935–1945
Bob Hyland (C), Boston College	1967–1969, 1976

I

Tunch Ilkin (T), Indiana State	1993
Ken Iman (C), Southeast Missouri State	1960–1963
Bob Ingalls (C-LB), Michigan	1942
Darryl Ingram (TE), California	1992–1993
Mark Ingram (WR), Michigan State	1995
Cecil Isbell (B), Purdue	1938–1942
Eddie Lee Ivery (RB), Georgia Tech	1979–1986

J

Chris Jacke (K), Texas–El Paso	1989–1996
Alcender Jackson (G), LSU	2002
Chris Jackson (WR), Washington State	2002–2003
Grady Jackson (DT), Knoxville	2003–2005
James Jackson (RB), Miami (Florida)	2004
Johnnie Jackson (S), Houston	1992
Keith Jackson (TE), Oklahoma	1995–1996
Mel Jackson (G), USC	1976–1980
Allen Jacobs (HB), Utah	1965
Jack Jacobs (B), Oklahoma	1947–1949
Harry Jacunski (E), Fordham	1939–1944
Van Jakes (CB), Kent State	1989
Claudis James (WR), Jackson State	1967–1968
Ernie Janet (G), Washington	1975

Ed Jankowski (B), Wisconsin	1937–1941	Steve Josue (LB), Carson-Newman	2004
Val Jansante (E), Duquesne	1951	Seth Joyner (LB), Texas–El Paso	1997
Craig Jay (TE), Mount Senario	1987	Bhawoh Jue (CB-S), Penn State	2001–2004
John Jefferson (WR), Arizona State	1981–1984	John Jurkovic (NT), Eastern Illinois	1991–1995
Norman Jefferson (DB), LSU	1987–1988		
Ray Jenison (T), South Dakota State	1931	**K**	
Noel Jenke (LB), Minnesota	1973–1974	Bob Kahler (B), Nebraska	1942–1944
Billy Jenkins (S), Howard	2001	Royal Kahler (T), Nebraska	1942
Cullen Jenkins (DT-DE), Central Michigan	2004–2005	Aaron Kampman (DE), Iowa	2002–2005
Jim Jennings (E), Missouri	1955	Leo Katalinas (T), Catholic University	1938
Greg Jensen (G), No College	1987	Kani Kauahi (C), Hawaii	1988
Jim Jensen (RB), Iowa	1981–1982	Jim Keane (E), Iowa	1952
Travis Jervey (RB), Citadel	1995–1998	Emmett Keefe (T), Notre Dame	1921
Bob Jeter (DB), Iowa	1963–1970	Jim Kekeris (T), Missouri	1948
Bill Johnson (DE), Minnesota	1941	Paul Kell (T), Notre Dame	1939–1940
Charles Johnson (DT), Maryland	1979–1980, 1983	Bill Kelley (E), Texas Tech	1949
Danny Johnson (LB), Tennessee State	1978	Joe Kelly (LB), Washington	1995
Ezra Johnson (DE), Morris Brown	1977–1987	Perry Kemp (WR), California	
Glenn Johnson (T), Arizona State	1949	(Pennsylvania)	1988–1991
Howard Johnson (G-LB), Georgia	1940–1941	Bob Kercher (DE), Georgetown	1944
Joe Johnson (HB), Boston College	1954–1958	Bill Kern (T), Pittsburgh	1929
Joe Johnson (DE), Louisville	2002–2003	Ken Keuper (B), Georgia	1945–1947
Kenneth Johnson (DB), Mississippi State	1987	Blair Kiel (QB), Notre Dame	1988–1991
KeShon Johnson (CB), Arizona	1994, 1997	Walt Kiesling (G), St. Thomas	1935–1936
LeShon Johnson (RB), Northern Illinois	1994–1995	Kelvin Kight (WR-KR), Florida	2004
Marvin Johnson (DB), San Jose State	1952–1953	Warren Kilbourne (T), Minnesota	1939
Randy Johnson (QB), Texas A&I	1976	Bobby Kimball (WR), Oklahoma	1979–1980
Reggie Johnson (TE), Florida State	1994, 1997	J. D. Kimmel (DT), Houston	1958
Sammy Johnson (RB), North Carolina	1979	Billy Kinard (B), Mississippi	1957–1958
Tom Johnson (DT), Michigan	1952	Randy Kinder (DB), Notre Dame	1997
Chester Johnston (B), Marquette	1931, 1934–1938	David King (DB), Auburn	1987
Mike Jolly (S), Michigan	1980, 1982–1983	Don King (DT), Kentucky	1956
Bob Jones (G), Indiana	1934	Don King (DB), SMU	1987
Boyd Jones (T), Texas Southern	1984	Jack Kirby (B), USC	1949
Bruce Jones (G), Alabama	1927–1928	Syd Kitson (G), Wake Forest	1980–1981, 1983–1984
Calvin Jones (RB), Nebraska	1996	Jim Kitts (FB), Ferrum	1998
Darryl Jones (DB), Georgia	1984–1985	Fee Klaus (C), No College	1921
Jamal Jones (WR-KR), North Carolina (A&T)	2005	Adrian Klemm (G), Hawaii	2005
Ron Jones (TE), Texas–El Paso	1969	Adolph Kliebhan (B), No College	1921
Scott Jones (T), Washington	1991	Gary Knafelc (E), Colorado	1954–1962
Sean Jones (DE), Northeastern	1994–1996	Lindsay Knapp (G), Notre Dame	1996
Terry Jones (NT), Alabama	1978–1984	Gene Knutson (DE), Michigan	1954, 1956
Tom Jones (G), Bucknell	1938	Steve Knutson (T), USC	1976–1977
Charles Jordan (WR), Long		Matt Koart (DE), USC	1986
Beach City	1994–1995, 1999	Greg Koch (T), Arkansas	1977–1985
Henry Jordan (DT), Virginia	1959–1969	Mark Koncar (T), Colorado	1976–1977,
Kenneth Jordan (LB), Tuskegee	1987		1979–1981
Carl Jorgensen (T), St. Mary's (California)	1934	Ed Konopasek (T), Ball State	1987

George Koonce (LB), East Carolina	1992–1999
Dave Kopay (RB), Washington	1972
Ron Kostelnik (T), Cincinnati	1961–1968
Eddie Kotal (B), Lawrence	1925–1929
John Kovatch (E), Notre Dame	1947
Bob Kowalkowski (G), Virginia	1977
Jerry Kramer (G), Idaho	1958–1968
Ron Kramer (TE), Michigan	1957, 1959–1964
Keneth Kranz (B), Milwaukee Teachers	1949
Larry Krause (RB), St. Norbert	1970–1971, 1973–1974
Bob Kroll (S), Northern Michigan	1972–1973
Bob Kuberski (DT), Navy	1995–1998
Rudy Kuechenberg (LB), Indiana	1970
Joe Kurth (T), Notre Dame	1933–1934
Bill Kuusisto (G), Minnesota	1941–1946

L

Matt LaBounty (DE), Oregon	1995
Wally Ladrow (HB), No College	1921
Bob Lally (LB), Cornell	1976
Curly Lambeau (B), Notre Dame	1921–1929
Pete Lammons (TE), Texas	1972
Cliff Lande (E), Carroll	1921
Walt Landers (FB), Clark	1978–1979
Sean Landeta (P), Towson State	1998
MacArthur Lane (RB), Utah State	1972–1974
Jim Lankas (FB), St. Mary's (California)	1943
Bill Larson (TE), Colorado State	1980
Fred Larson (C), Notre Dame	1925
Kurt Larson (LB), Michigan State	1991
Jim Laslavic (LB), Penn State	1982
Kit Lathrop (DT), Arizona State	1979–1980
Dutch Lauer (E), Detroit	1922
Larry Lauer (C), Alabama	1956–1957
Jim Laughlin (LB), Ohio State	1983
Jim Lawrence (B), TCU	1939
Joe Laws (B), Iowa	1934–1935
Vonta Leach (FB), East Carolina	2004–2005
John Leake (LB), Clemson	2005
Wes Leaper (E), Wisconsin	1921, 1923
Bill Lee (T), Alabama	1937–1942, 1946
Charles Lee (WR), Central Florida	2000–2001
Donald Lee (TE), Mississippi State	2005
James Lee (DT), Oregon State	2004
Mark Lee (CB), Washington	1980–1990
ReShard Lee (RB), Middle Tennessee State	2005
Charlie Leigh (RB), No College	1974

Tony Leiker (DE), Stanford	1987
Walt LeJeune (G), Heidelberg	1925–1926
Paris Lenon (LB), Richmond	2002–2005
Bobby Leopold (LB), Notre Dame	1986
Darrell Lester (C), TCU	1937–1938
Russ Letlow (G), San Francisco	1936–1942, 1946
Dorsey Levens (RB), Georgia Tech	1994–2001
Verne Lewellen (B), Nebraska	1924–1932
Cliff Lewis (LB), Southern Mississippi	1981–1984
Gary Lewis (TE), Texas-Arlington	1981–1984
Mark Lewis (TE), Texas A&M	1985–1987
Mike Lewis (NT), Arkansas A&M	1980
Ron Lewis (WR), Florida State	1992–1994
Tim Lewis (CB), Pittsburgh	1983–1986
Carl Lidberg (FB), Minnesota	1926, 1929–1930
Paul Lipscomb (T), Tennessee	1945–1949
Earl Little (S), Miami (Florida)	2005
Dale Livingston (K), Western Michigan	1970
James Lofton (WR), Stanford	1978–1986
David Logan (NT), Pittsburgh	1987
Dick Logan (G), Ohio State	1952–1953
Slick Lollar (FB), Samford	1928
Antonio London (LB), Alabama	1998
Bob Long (WR), Wichita	1964–1967
Ryan Longwell (K), California	1997–2005
Ace Loomis (B), La Crosse St. Teachers	1951–1953
Jack Losch (HB), Miami (Florida)	1956
Chad Lucas (WR), Alabama State	2005
Nick Luchey (FB), Miami (Florida)	2003–2004
Bill Lucky (DT), Baylor	1955
Bill Lueck (G), Arizona	1968–1974
Nolan Luhn (E), Tulsa	1945–1949
Steve Luke (DB), Ohio State	1975–1980
Booth Lusteg (K), Connecticut	1969
Dewey Lyle (E), Minnesota	1922–1923
Del Lyman (T), UCLA	1941
Billy Lyon (DT-DE), Marshall	1998–2002

M

Bill Maas (NT), Pittsburgh	1993
Red Mack (WR), Notre Dame	1966
Tom MacLeod (LB), Minnesota	1973
George Maddox (T), Kansas State	1935
Don Majkowski (QB), Virginia	1987–1992
Rydell Malancon (LB), LSU	1987
Grover Malone (B), Notre Dame	1921
Tony Mandarich (T), Michigan State	1989–1991
Chris Mandeville (DB), California-Davis	1987–1988

Leon Manley (G), Oklahoma	1950–1951
Bob Mann (E), Michigan	1950–1954
Errol Mann (K), North Dakota	1968, 1976
Brian Manning (WR), Stanford	1998
Roy Manning (LB), Michigan	2005
Von Mansfield (DB), Wisconsin	1987
Chester Marcol (K), Hillsdale	1972–1980
Larry Marks (B), Indiana	1928
Rich Marshall (DT), Stephen F. Austin	1965
Torrance Marshall (LB-FB), Oklahoma	2001–2004
Herman Martell (E), No College	1921
Charles Martin (DE), Livingston	1984–1987
David Martin (TE), Tennessee	2001–2005
John Martinkovic (DE), Xavier	1951–1956
Russell Maryland (DE), Miami (Florida)	2000
Dave Mason (DB), Nebraska	1974
Joel Mason (E), Western Michigan	1942–1945
Larry Mason (RB), Troy State	1988
Carlton Massey (DT), Texas	1957–1958
Norm Masters (T), Michigan State	1957–1964
Stan Mataele (NT), Oklahoma	1987
Charlie Mathys (B), Indiana	1922–1926
Pat Matson (G), Oregon	1975
Al Matthews (DB), Texas A&I	1970–1975
Aubrey Matthews (WR), Delta State	1988–1989
Harry Mattos (B), St. Mary's (California)	1936
Marv Matuszak (LB), Tulsa	1958
Frank Mayer (G), Notre Dame	1927
Derrick Mayes (WR), Notre Dame	1996–1998
Kivuusama Mays (LB), North Carolina	1999
Jack McAuliffe (HB), Beloit	1926
Ron McBride (RB), Missouri	1973
Tod McBride (CB-S), UCLA	1999–2002
Bob McCaffrey (C), USC	1975
Larry McCarren (C), Illinois	1973–1984
Eugene McCaslin (LB), Florida	2000
Dave McCloughan (CB), Colorado	1992
Phil McConkey (WR), Navy	1986
Mike McCoy (DB), Colorado	1976–1983
Mike McCoy (DT), Notre Dame	1970–1976
Hurdis McCrary (B), Georgia	1929–1933
Dustin McDonald (G), Indiana	1935
Bob McDougal (B), Miami (Florida)	1947
John McDowell (G), St. John's (Minnesota)	1964
Blaine McElmurry (S), Montana	1997
Scott McGarrahan (S), New Mexico	1998–2000
John McGarry (G), St. Joseph's	1987
Walter McGaw (G), Beloit	1926

Clarence McGeary (DT), North Dakota State	1950
Buford McGee (FB), Mississippi	1992
Max McGee (E), Tulane	1954, 1957–1967
Rich McGeorge (TE), Elon	1970–1978
Lenny McGill (CB), Arizona State	1994–1995
Sylvester McGrew (DE), Tulane	1987
Michael McGruder (CB), Kent State	1989
Gene McGuire (C), Notre Dame	1996
Lamar McHan (QB), Arkansas	1959–1960
Sean McHugh (TE), Penn State	2004
Don McIlhenny (HB), SMU	1957–1959
Guy McIntyre (G), Georgia	1994
Paul McJulien (P), Jackson State	1991–1992
Roy McKay (B), Texas	1944–1947
Keith McKenzie (DE-LB), Ball State	1996–1999, 2002
Mike McKenzie (CB), Memphis	1999–2004
Raleigh McKenzie (G), Tennessee	1999–2000
Joe McLaughlin (LB), Massachusetts	1979
Lee McLaughlin (G), Virginia	1941
Ray McLean (B), No College	1921
Mike McLeod (DB), Montana State	1984–1985
Jim McMahon (QB), BYU	1995–1996
Herb McMath (DT), Morningside	1977
Steve McMichael (DT), Texas	1994
Ernie McMillan (T), Illinois	1975
Dexter McNab (RB), Florida	1992–1993
Johnny McNally (B), St. John's	1929–1933, 1935–1936
Forrest McPherson (T), Nebraska	1943–1945
Mike Meade (FB), Penn State	1982–1983
Rondell Mealey (RB), LSU	2001–2002
Steve Mellinger (E), Kentucky	1958, 1960
James Melka (LB), Wisconsin	1987
Ruben Mendoza (G), Wayne State	1986
Chuck Mercein (RB), Yale	1967–1969
Mike Mercer (K), Northern Arizona	1968–1969
Casey Merrill (DE), California-Davis	1979–1983
Mark Merrill (LB), Minnesota	1982
Mike Merriweather (LB), Pacific	1993
Frank Mestnik (FB), Marquette	1963
Eric Metcalf (RB-KR), Texas	2002
Jim Meyer (T), Illinois State	1987
Lou Michaels (K), Kentucky	1971
Walt Michaels (G), Washington & Lee	1951
Mike Michalske (G), Penn State	1929–1935, 1937
John Michels (T), USC	1996–1997
Terry Mickens (WR), Florida A&M	1994–1997
Terdell Middleton (RB), Memphis State	1977–1981

Lou Midler (DE), Minnesota	1940
Lou Mihajlovich (DE), Indiana	1954
Don Milan (QB), Cal Poly–San Luis Obispo	1975
Keith Millard (DE), Washington State	1992
Don Miller (B), Wisconsin	1941–1942
Don Miller (B), SMU	1954
John Miller (T), Boston College	1960
John Miller (LB), Mississippi State	1987
Ookie Miller (C), Purdue	1938
Paul Miller (B), South Dakota State	1936–1938
Tom Miller (E), Hampden-Sydney	1946
Stan Mills (B), Penn State	1922–1923
Paul Minick (G), Iowa	1928–1929
Basil Mitchell (RB), TCU	1999–2000
Charles Mitchell (B), Tulsa	1946
Roland Mitchell (CB-S), Texas Tech	1991–1994
Mike Mofitt (WR), Fresno State	1996
Dick Moje (E), Loyola (California)	1951
Bo Molenda (B), Michigan	1928–1932
Ron Monaco (LB), South Carolina	1987
Bob Monnett (B), Michigan State	1933–1938
Henry Monroe (DB), Mississippi State	1979
Michael Montgomery (DE), Texas A&M	2005
Allen Moore (E), Texas A&M	1939
Blake Moore (C-G), Wooster	1984–1985
Brent Moore (DE), USC	1987
Jason Moore (S), San Diego State	2002
Rich Moore (DT), Villanova	1969–1970
Tom Moore (HB), Vanderbilt	1960–1965
Rich Moran (G), San Diego State	1985–1993
Tim Moresco (DB), Syracuse	1977
Anthony Morgan (WR), Tennessee	1993–1996
Steve Morley (G), St. Mary's (Canada)	2004
Jim Bob Morris (DB), Kansas State	1987
Larry Morris (RB), Syracuse	1987
Lee Morris (WR), Oklahoma	1987
Jim Morrissey (LB), Michigan State	1993
Mike Morton (LB), North Carolina	2000
J. J. Moses (WR-KR), Iowa State	2002
Dom Moselle (B), Superior State	1951–1952
Russ Mosely (B), Alabama	1945–1946
Perry Moss (QB), Illinois	1948
Joe Mott (LB), Iowa	1993
Norm Mott (B), Georgia	1933
Roderick Mullen (CB-S), Grambling State	1995–1997
Carl Mulleneaux (E), Utah State	1938–1941, 1945–1946
Lee Mulleneaux (C), Northern Arizona	1938

Mark Murphy (S), West Liberty State	1980–1985, 1987–1991
Jab Murray (T), Marquette	1921–1924
Terrence Murray (WR), Texas A&M	2005

N

Romanus Nadolney (G), Notre Dame	1922
Craig Nall (QB), Northwestern (Louisiana) State	2003–2004
Tom Nash (E), Georgia	1928–1932
Hannibal Navies (LB), Colorado	2003–2004
Ed Neal (DT-T), Tulane	1945–1951
Frankie Neal (WR), Fort Hays State	1987
Bill Neill (NT), Pittsburgh	1984
Bob Nelson (NT), Miami (Florida)	1988–1990
Jim Nelson (LB), Penn State	1998–1999
Tom Neville (T-G), Fresno State	1986–1988, 1992
Craig Newsome (CB), Arizona State	1995–1998
Hamilton Nichols (G), Rice	1951
Hardy Nickerson (LB), California	2000
Walter Niemann (C), Michigan	1922–1923
Ray Nitschke (LB), Illinois	1958–1972
Doyle Nix (DB), SMU	1955
Fred Nixon (WR), Oklahoma	1980–1981
Brian Noble (LB), Arizona State	1985–1993
Danny Noonan (NT), Nebraska	1992
Al Norgard (E), Stanford	1934
Mike Norseth (QB), Kansas	1990
Jerry Norton (DB), SMU	1963–1964
Marty Norton (B), Hamline	1925
Rick Norton (QB), Kentucky	1970
Bob Nussbaumer (B), Michigan	1946, 1951
Rick Nuzum (C), Kentucky	1987
Chukie Nwokorie (DE), Purdue	2003
Lee Nystrom (T), Macalester	1974

O

Bill Oakes (T), Haskell	1921
Brad Oates (T), BYU	1981
Carleton Oats (DT), Florida A&M	1973
Harry O'Boyle (B), Notre Dame	1928, 1932
Bob O'Connor (T), Stanford	1935
Steve Odom (WR), Utah	1974–1979
Pat O'Donahue (DE), Wisconsin	1955
Dick O'Donnell (E), Minnesota	1924–1930
Urban Odson (T), Minnesota	1946–1949
Alfred Oglesby (NT), Houston	1992
Earl Ohlgren (DE), Minnesota	1942

Steve Okoniewski (DT), Montana	1974–1975
Muhammad Oliver (CB), Oregon	1993
Ralph Olsen (E), Utah	1949
Larry Olsonoski (G), Minnesota	1948–1949
Tom O'Malley (QB), Cincinnati	1950
Andre O'Neal (LB), Marshall	2001
Ed O'Neill (LB), Penn State	1980
Dan Orlich (E), Nevada	1949–1951
Dave Osborn (RB), North Dakota	1976
Dwayne O'Steen (CB), San Jose State	1983–1984
J. T. O'Sullivan (QB), California-Davis	2004
Rip Owens (G), Lawrence	1922

P

Sam Palumbo (LB-C), Notre Dame	1957
Ernie Pannell (T), Texas A&M	1941–1942, 1945
Orrin Pape (B), Iowa	1930
Johnny Papit (HB), Virginia	1953
Babe Parilli (QB), Kentucky	1952–1953, 1957–1958
De'Mond Parker (RB), Oklahoma	1999–2000
Freddie Parker (RB), Mississippi Valley State	1987
Chet Parlavecchio (LB), Penn State	1983
Keith Paskett (WR), Western Kentucky	1987
George Paskavan (B), Wisconsin	1941
Frank Patrick (QB), Nebraska	1970–1972
Shawn Patterson (DE), Arizona State	1988–1991, 1993
Ricky Patton (RB), Jackson State	1979
Tony Paulekas (C), Washington & Jefferson	1936
Bryce Paup (LB), Northern Iowa	1990–1994
Ken Payne (WR), Langston	1974–1977
Lindell Pearson (HB), Oklahoma	1952
Francis Peay (T), Missouri	1968–1972
Doug Pederson (QB), Northeast Louisiana	1996–1998, 2001–2004
Ray Pelfrey (E), Eastern Kentucky	1951–1952
Don Perkins (FB), Platteville St. Teachers	1944–1945
Tom Perko (LB), Pittsburgh	1976
Claude Perry (T), Alabama	1927–1935
Dick Pesonen (DB), Minnesota-Duluth	1960
Kenny Peterson (DT), Ohio State	2003–2005
Les Peterson (E), Texas	1932, 1934
Ray Peterson (B), San Francisco	1937
John Petitbon (DB), Notre Dame	1957
David Petway (S), Northern Illinois	1981
Bruce Pickens (CB), Nebraska	1993
Steve Pisarkiewicz (QB), Missouri	1980
Elijah Pitts (RB), Philander Smith	1961–1969, 1971

Ron Pitts (CB), UCLA	1988–1990
Kurt Ploeger (DE), Gustavus Adolphus	1986
John Pointer (LB), Vanderbilt	1987
Bucky Pope (WR), Catawba	1968
Brady Poppinga (LB), Brigham Young	2005
Sammy Powers (G), No College	1921
Guy Prather (LB), Grambling State	1981–1985
Merv Pregulman (G), Michigan	1946
Harold Prescott (E), Hardin-Simmons	1946
Roell Preston (WR-KR), Mississippi	1997–1998
Mike Prior (S), Illinois State	1993–1998
Steve Pritko (E), Villanova	1949–1950
Joe Prokop (P), Cal Poly–Pomona	1985
Fred Provo (B), Washington	1948
Jim Psaltis (DB), USC	1954
Pid Purdy (B), Beloit	1926–1927
Dave Pureifory (DL), Eastern Michigan	1972–1977
Frank Purnell (FB), Alcorn A&M	1957

Q

Jes Quatse (T), Pittsburgh	1933
Jeff Query (WR), Millikin	1989–1991
Bill Quinlan (DE), Michigan State	1959–1962

R

Ken Radick (E), Marquette	1930–1931
Vince Rafferty (C), Colorado	1987
Al Randolph (DB), Iowa	1971
Terry Randolph (DB), American International	1977
Keith Ranspot (E), SMU	1942
Lou Rash (DB), Mississippi Valley State	1987
Baby Ray (T), Vanderbilt	1938–1948
Cornelius Redick (WR), Cal State–Fullerton	1987
Pete Regnier (B), Minnesota	1922
Bill Reichardt (FB), Iowa	1952
Floyd Reid (HB), Georgia	1950–1956
Bill Renner (P), Virginia	1986–1987
Jamal Reynolds (DE), Florida State	2001–2003
Jay Rhodemyer (C-LB), Kentucky	1948–1949, 1951–1952
Allen Rice (RB), Baylor	1991
Gary Richard (DB), Pittsburgh	1998
Ray Riddick (E), Fordham	1940–1942, 1946
Jim Ringo (C), Syracuse	1953–1963
Alan Risher (QB), LSU	1987

Andre Rison (WR), Michigan State	1996
Marco Rivera (G), Penn State	1997–2004
John Roach (QB), SMU	1961–1963
Austin Robbins (DT), North Carolina	2000
Tootie Robbins (T), East Carolina	1992–1993
Bill Roberts (HB), Dartmouth	1956
Bill Robinson (HB), Lincoln (Missouri)	1952
Charley Robinson (G), Morgan State	1951
Dave Robinson (LB), Penn State	1963–1972
Eugene Robinson (S), Colgate	1996–1997
Michael Robinson (CB), Hampton	1996
Tommy Robison (G), Texas A&M	1987
Alden Roche (DE), Southern	1971–1976
Aaron Rodgers (QB), California	2005
Del Rodgers (RB), Utah	1982, 1984
Nick Rogers (LB), Georgia Tech	2004
Herman Rohrig (B), Nebraska	1941, 1946–1947
Dave Roller (DT), Kentucky	1975–1978
Mark Roman (S), LSU	2004–2005
Al Romine (HB), Alabama	1955, 1958
Rudy Rosatti (T), Michigan	1924, 1926–1927
Al Rose (E), Texas	1932–1936
Bob Rose (C), Ripon	1926
Gus Rosenow (B), Wisconsin	1921
Ken Roskie (B), South Carolina	1948
Dan Ross (TE), Northeastern	1986
Allen Rossum (CB-KR), Notre Dame	2000–2001
Tobin Rote (QB), Rice	1950–1956
John Rowser (DB), Michigan	1967–1969
Larry Rubens (C), Montana State	1982–1983
T. J. Rubley (QB), Tulsa	1995
Paul Rudzinski (LB), Michigan State	1978–1980
Grey Ruegamer (C-G), Arizona State	2003–2005
Ken Ruettgers (T), USC	1985–1996
Howard Ruetz (DT), Loras	1951–1953
Gordon Rule (DB), Dartmouth	1968–1969
Clive Rush (E), Miami (Ohio)	1953
Steve Ruzich (G), Ohio State	1952–1954

S

Harvey Salem (T), California	1992
Jim Salisbury (G), UCLA	1957–1958
Chuck Sample (B), Toledo	1942, 1945
Howard Sampson (DB), Arkansas	1978–1979
Ron Sams (G), Pittsburgh	1983
B. J. Sander (P), Ohio State	2005
Dan Sandider (B), LSU	1952–1953
Terdell Sands (DT), Tennessee-Chattanooga	2003

John Sandusky (T), Villanova	1956
Al Sarafiny (C), St. Edwards'	1933
Brian Satterfield (FB), North Alabama	1996
George Sauer (B), Nebraska	1935–1937
Russ Saunders (FB), USC	1931
Hurles Scales (DB), North Texas State	1975
Francis Schammel (G), Iowa	1937
Bernie Scherer (E), Nebraska	1936–1938
Walt Schlinkman (FB), Texas Tech	1946–1949
Art Schmaehl (FB), No College	1921
George Schmidt (C), Lewis	1952
John Schmidtt (C), Hofstra	1974
Herm Schneidman (B), Iowa	1935–1939
Roy Schoemann (C), Marquette	1938
Bill Schroeder (WR), Wisconsin-La Crosse	1994, 1997–2001
Charles Schroll (G), LSU	1951
Carl Schuette (C-DB), Marquette	1950–1951
Harry Schuh (T), Memphis State	1974
Jeff Schuh (LB), Minnesota	1986
Charles Schultz (T), Minnesota	1939–1940
Ade Schwammel (T), Oregon State	1934–1936, 1943–1944
Patrick Scott (WR), Grambling State	1987–1988
Randy Scott (LB), Alabama	1981–1986
Bucky Scribner (P), Kansas	1983–1984
Joe Secord (C), No College	1922
George Seeman (E), Nebraska	1940
Champ Seibold (T), Wisconsin	1934–1938, 1940
Clarence Self (B), Wisconsin	1952, 1954–1955
Wash Serini (G), Kentucky	1952
Jim Shanley (HB), Oregon	1958
Sterling Sharpe (WR), South Carolina	1988–1994
Darren Sharper (CB-S), William & Mary	1997–2004
Dexter Shelley (B), Texas	1932
Joe Shield (QB), Trinity (Connecticut)	1986
Fred Shirey (T), Nebraska	1940
Mark Shumate (NT), Wisconsin	1985
Vai Sikahema (RB-KR), BYU	1991
Davie Simmons (LB), North Carolina	1979
John Simmons (DB), SMU	1986
Wayne Simmons (LB), Clemson	1993–1997
Ron Simpkins (LB), Michigan	1988
Nate Simpson (RB), Tennessee State	1977–1979
Travis Simpson (C), Oklahoma	1987
Joe Sims (T-G), Nebraska	1992–1995
Reggie Singletary (T), North Carolina State	1991
Daryle Skaugstad (NT), California	1993

Gil Skeate (FB), Gonzaga	1927
Joe Skibinski (G), Purdue	1955–1956
Gerald Skinner (T), Arkansas	1978
Bob Skoglund (DE), Notre Dame	1947
Bob Skoronski (T), Indiana	1956,
	1959–1968
T. J. Slaughter (LB), Southern Mississippi	2003
Elmer Sleight (T), Purdue	1930–1931
Barry Smith (WR), Florida State	1973–1975
Barty Smith (RB), Richmond	1974–1980
Ben Smith (E), Alabama	1933
Blane Smith (LB), Purdue	1977
Bruce Smith (B), Minnesota	1945–1948
Donnell Smith (DE), Southern	1971
Earl Smith (E), Ripon	1922
Ed Smith (B), New York University	1937
Ed Smith (HB), Texas Mines	1948–1949
Ernie Smith (T), USC	1935–1937, 1939
Jermaine Smith (DT), Georgia	1997, 1999
Jerry Smith (G), Wisconsin	1956
Kevin Smith (FB), UCLA	1996
Larry Smith (DT-DE), Florida State	2003–2004
Moe Smith (RB), North Carolina A&T	2002
Ollie Smith (WR), Tennessee State	1976–1977
Perry Smith (DB), Colorado State	1973–1976
Red Smith (G), Notre Dame	1927, 1929
Rex Smith (E), Wisconsin Teachers	1922
Rod Smith (CB), Notre Dame	1998
Warren Smith (G), Western Michigan	1921
Wes Smith (WR), East Texas State	1987
Ken Snelling (B), UCLA	1945
Malcolm Snider (T-G), Stanford	1972–1974
Matt Snider (FB), Richmond	1999–2000
Glen Sorenson (G), Utah State	1943–1945
John Spagnola (TE), Yale	1989
Al Sparlis (G), UCLA	1946
Ron Spears (DE), San Diego State	1983
Joe Spencer (T), Oklahoma A&M	1950–1951
Ollie Spencer (T), Kansas	1957–1958
John Spilis (WR), Northern Illinois	1969–1971
Jack Spinks (G), Alcorn A&M	1955–1956
Marcus Spriggs (T), Houston	2003
Dennis Sproul (QB), Arizona State	1978
Ray Stachowicz (P), Michigan State	1981–1982
Jon Staggers (WR), Missouri	1972–1974
Dick Stahlman (T), DePaul	1931–1932
Walter Stanley (WR), Mesa State	1985–1988
Don Stansauk (T), Denver	1950–1951

Ken Starch (RB), Wisconsin	1976
Paul Staroba (WR), Michigan	1973
Bart Starr (QB), Alabama	1956–1971
Ben Starret (B), St. Mary's (California)	1942–1945
Ben Steele (TE), Mesa State	2004–2005
Frank Steen (E), Rice	1939
Rebel Steiner (DB), Alabama	1950–1951
Jan Stenerud (K), Montana State	1980–1983
Scott Stephen (LB), Arizona State	1987–1991
John Stephens (RB), Northwest (Louisiana) State	1993
Dave Stephenson (G-C), West Virginia	1951–1955
John Sterling (RB), Central Oklahoma	1987
Bill Stevens (QB), Texas–El Paso	1968–1969
Steve Stewart (LB), Minnesota	1979
Ken Stills (S), Wisconsin	1985–1989
Barry Stokes (G-T), Eastern Michigan	2000–2001
Tim Stokes (T), Oregon	1978–1982
John Stonebreaker (E), USC	1942
Fred Strickland (LB), Purdue	1994–1995
Lyle Sturgeon (T), North Dakota State	1937
Carl Sullivan (DE), San Jose State	1987
John Sullivan (DB), California	1986
Walter Sullivan (G), Beloit	1921
Bob Summerhays (B), Utah	1949–1951
Don Summers (TE), Boise State	1987
Mickey Sutton (CB), Montana	1989
Earl Svendsen (C-LB), Minnesota	1935–1937, 1940–1941
Karl Swanke (T-C), Boston College	1980–1986
Erwin Swiney (CB), Nebraska	2002–2003
Veryl Switzer (B), Kansas State	1954–1955
Harry Sydney (FB), Kansas	1992
John Symank (DB), Florida	1957–1962
Len Szafaryn (T), North Carolina	1950, 1953–1956

T

Jerry Tagge (QB), Nebraska	1972–1974
Damon Tassos (G), Texas A&M	1947–1949
Claude Taugher (FB), Marquette	1922
Mark Tauscher (T-G), Wisconsin	2000–2005
Aaron Taylor (G), Notre Dame	1995–1997
Cliff Taylor (RB), Memphis State	1976
Jim Taylor (FB), LSU	1958–1966
Kitrick Taylor (WR), Washington State	1992
Lenny Taylor (WR), Tennessee	1984
Willie Taylor (WR), Pittsburgh	1978
George Teague (S), Alabama	1993–1995

Jim Temp (DE), Wisconsin	1957–1960
Bob Tenner (E), Minnesota	1935
Pat Terrell (S), Notre Dame	1978
Deral Teteak (LB-G), Wisconsin	1952–1956
Keith Thibodeaux (CB), Northwestern (Louisiana) State	2001
John Thierry (DE), Alcorn State	2000–2001
Ben Thomas (DE), Auburn	1986
Ike Thomas (DB), Bishop	1972–1973
Joey Thomas (CB), Montana State	2004–2005
Lavale Thomas (RB), Fresno State	1987–1988
Robert Thomas (LB), UCLA	2005
Bobby Thomason (QB), Virginia Military	1951
Jeff Thomason (TE), Oregon	1995–1999
Arland Thompson (G), Baylor	1981
Aundra Thompson (WR), East Texas State	1977–1981
Clarence Thompson (B), Minnesota	1939
Darrell Thompson (RB), Minnesota	1990–1994
John Thompson (TE), Utah State	1979–1982
Jeremy Thornburg (S), Northern Arizona	2005
Andrae Thurman (WR), Southern Oregon	2004–2005
Fuzzy Thurston (G), Valparaiso	1959–1967
George Timberlake (LB-G), USC	1955
Adam Timmerman (G), South Dakota State	1995–1998
Gerald Tinker (WR), Kent State	1975
Pete Tinsley (G-LB), Georgia	1938–1939, 1941–1945
Nelson Toburen (LB), Wichita State	1961–1962
Chuck Tollefson (G), Iowa	1944–1946
Mike Tomczak (QB), Ohio State	1991
Jared Tomich (DE), Nebraska	2002
Tom Toner (LB), Idaho State	1973, 1975–1977
Clayton Tonnemaker (LB-C), Minnesota	1950, 1953–1954
Eric Torkelson (RB), Connecticut	1974–1979, 1981
Keith Traylor (LB), Central Oklahoma	1993
Bill Troup (QB), South Carolina	1980
R-Kal Truluck (DE), Cortland State	2004
Esera Tuaolo (NT-DE), Oregon State	1991–1992
Walter Tullis (WR), Delaware State	1978–1979
Emlen Tunnell (S), Iowa	1959–1961
Maurice Turner (RB), Utah State	1985
Rich Turner (NT), Oklahoma	1981–1983
Wylie Turner (DB), Angelo State	1979–1980
Miles Turpin (LB), California	1986
George Tuttle (E), Minnesota	1927
Francis Twedell (G), Minnesota	1939

U

Keith Uecker (G-T), Auburn	1984–1985, 1987–1988, 1990–1991
Marviel Underwood (S), San Diego State	2005
Andy Uram (B), Minnesota	1938–1943
Alex Urban (E), South Carolina	1941, 1944–1945
Eddie Usher (B), Michigan	1922, 1924

V

Dominic Vairo (E), Notre Dame	1935
Phil Vandersea (LB-DE), Massachusetts	1966, 1968–1969
Bruce Van Dyke (G), Missouri	1974–1976
Hal Van Every (B), Minnesota	1940–1941
Vernon Vanoy (DT), Kansas	1972
Clyde Van Sickle (C), Arkansas	1932–1933
Fred Vant Hull (G), Minnesota	1942
Pete Van Valkenberg (RB), BYU	1974
Randy Vataha (WR), Stanford	1977
Alan Veingrad (T), East Texas State	1986–1987, 1989–1990
Ross Verba (T-G), Iowa	1997–2000
Carl Vereen (T), Georgia Tech	1957
George Vergara (E), Notre Dame	1925
David Viaene (T), Minnesota-Duluth	1992
Vince Villanucci (NT), Bowling Green	1987
Fred Vinson (CB), Vanderbilt	1999
Evan Vogds (G), Wisconsin	1948–1949
Lloyd Voss (DT), Nebraska	1964–1965
Walter Voss (E), Detroit	1925

W

Jude Waddy (LB), William & Mary	1998–1999
Charlie Wade (WR), Tennessee State	1975
Carl Wafer (DT), Tennessee State	1974
Bryan Wagner (P), Cal State–Northridge	1992–1993
Buff Wagner (B), Carroll (Wisconsin)	1921
Steve Wagner (DB), Wisconsin	1976–1979
Mike Wahle (T-G), Navy	1998–2004
Cleo Walker (C-LB), Louisville	1970
Javon Walker (WR), Florida State	2002–2005
Malcolm Walker (C), Rice	1970
Randy Walker (P), Northwest (Louisiana) State	1974
Rod Walker (DT), Troy State	2001–2003
Sammy Walker (CB), Texas Tech	1993
Val Joe Walker (DB), SMU	1953–1956
Calvin Wallace (DE), West Virginia Tech	1987

Taco Wallace (WR), Kansas State	2005
Wesley Walls (TE), Mississippi	2003
Ward Walsh (RB), Colorado	1972
Steve Warren (DT), Nebraska	2000, 2002
Chuck Washington (DB), Arkansas	1987
Elbert Watts (DB), USC	1986
Nate Wayne (LB), Mississippi	2000–2002
Clarence Weathers (WR), Delaware State	1990–1991
Jim Weatherwax (DT), California State–L.A.	1966–1967, 1969
Gary Weaver (LB), Fresno State	1975–1979
Chuck Webb (RB), Tennessee	1987
Dutch Webber (E), Kansas State	1928
Tim Webster (K), Arkansas	1971
Mike Weddington (LB), Oklahoma	1986–1990
Ray Wehba (E), USC	1944
Lee Weigel (RB), Wisconsin–Eau Claire	1987
Dick Weisgerber (B), Williamette	1938–1940, 1942
Clayton Weishuhn (LB), Angelo State	1987
Mike Wellman (C), Kansas	1979–1980
Don Wells (E), Georgia	1946–1949
Scott Wells (C-G), Tennessee	2004–2005
Terry Wells (RB), Southern Mississippi	1975
Ed West (TE), Auburn	1984–1994
Pat West (B), USC	1948
Bryant Westbrook (CB), Texas	2003
Ryan Wetnight (TE), Stanford	2000
Lyle Wheeler (E), Ripon	1921–1923
Bill Whitaker (DB), Missouri	1981–1982
Adrian White (S), Florida	1992
Chris White (C), Southern Mississippi	2005
Gene White (DB), Georgia	1954
Reggie White (DE), Tennessee	1993–1998
David Whitehurst (QB), Furman	1977–1983
James Whitley (S), Michigan	2003–2004
Jesse Whittenton (DB), Texas Western	1958–1964
William Whitticker (G), Michigan State	2005
Bob Wicks (WR), Utah State	1974
Ron Widby (P), Tennessee	1972–1973
Doug Widell (G), Boston College	1993
Dick Wildung (T), Minnesota	1946–1951, 1953
Elmer Wilkens (E), Indiana	1925
Bruce Wilkerson (T), Tennessee	1996–1997
Gabe Wilkins (DE-DT), Gardner-Webb	1994–1997
Marcus Wilkins (LB), Texas	2002–2003
Kevin Willhite (RB), Oregon	1987
A. D. Williams (E), Pacific	1959
Brian Williams (LB), USC	1995–2000
Clarence Williams (DE), Prairie View A&M	1970–1977
Corey Williams (DE-DT), Arkansas State	2004–2005
Delvin Williams (RB), Kansas	1981
Gerald Williams (DE), Auburn	1987
Howard Williams (DB), Howard	1962–1963
K. D. Williams (LB), Henderson State	2000–2001
Kevin Williams (RB), UCLA	1993
Mark Williams (LB), Ohio State	1994
Perry Williams (RB), Purdue	1969–1973
Travis Williams (RB-KR), Arizona State	1967–1970
Tyrone Williams (CB), Nebraska	1996–2002
Walter Williams (RB), Grambling State	2004–2005
Matt Willig (T), USC	1998
James Willis (LB), Auburn	1993–1994
Jeff Wilner (TE), Wesleyan (Connecticut)	1994–1995
Ben Wilson (FB), USC	1967
Charles Wilson (WR), Memphis State	1990–1991
Faye Wilson (B), Texas A&M	1930–1931
Gene Wilson (E-DB), SMU	1947–1948
Marcus Wilson (RB), Virginia	1992–1995
Milt Wilson (G), Wisconsin Teachers	1921
Paul Wilson (WR), Texas–El Paso	1972
Ray Wilson (S), New Mexico	1994
Abner Wimberly (E), LSU	1950–1952
Blake Wingle (G), UCLA	1985
Rich Wingo (LB), Alabama	1979, 1981–1984
Francis Winkler (DE), Memphis State	1968–1969
Randy Winkler (G), Tarleton State	1971
Paul Winslow (HB), North Carolina Central	1960
Blaise Winter (DE-NT), Syracuse	1988–1990
Chet Winters (RB), Oklahoma	1983
Frank Winters (C-G), Western Illinois	1992–2002
Wimpy Winther (C), Mississippi	1971
Jerron Wishom (CB), Louisiana Tech	2005
Jerry Wisne (T), Notre Dame	2002
Cal Withrow (C), Kentucky	1971–1972
Earl Witte (B), Gustavus Adolphus	1934
Alex Wizbicki (B), Holy Cross	1950
Bobby Wood (T), Alabama	1940
Willie Wood (S), USC	1960–1971
Whitey Woodin (G), Marquette	1922–1931
Jerry Woods (S), Northern Michigan	1990
Keith Woodside (RB), Texas A&M	1988–1991
Vince Workman (RB), Ohio State	1989–1992
Keith Wortman (G), Nebraska	1972–1975
Randy Wright (QB), Wisconsin	1984–1988